# DOUBLE SCOTCH & WRY

D0756382

# *Double* ·SCOTCH· & ·WRY·

## Compiled by Gordon Menzies

Photographs by
Nigel Robertson and Tom Howat

BBC BOOKS

Published by BBC Books,
a division of BBC Enterprises Limited
Woodlands, 80 Wood Lane, London W12 0TT

First published 1988

© The Authors 1988

ISBN 0 563 20686 1

Set in 10/11 Aster by Ace Filmsetting Ltd, Frome, Somerset
Printed in Great Britain by Cambus Litho
Bound in Great Britain by Hunter and Foulis
Colour separations by Technik, Berkhamsted
Cover printed by Fletchers of Norwich

# CONTENTS

# FOREWORD

It is widely recognised that comedy is the biggest minefield in television. It is almost impossible to recommend a recipe for successful comedy. You need imaginative ideas, creative production and talented performers. But it all begins with the scripts. In some ways, the scriptwriters are the unsung heroes of television comedy. This book contains a selection of sketches from Scotland's most successful comedy show.

Writers, of course, are often frustrated when their ideas fail to reach fruition. In *Scotch & Wry* many of their ideas leap on to the screen because they are being realised and developed by a talented team of performers, headed by the incomparable Rikki Fulton.

Rikki Fulton has been a star of stage, screen and television for so long that he has become a Scottish institution. Arguably, he is the most famous Scottish entertainer since Harry Lauder; without doubt, he is the most versatile of all our showbiz stars. He has been admired in pantomine for more than thirty years, culminating in the 1987–88 *Cinderella* at the King's Theatre in Glasgow. That particular pantomime, starring Rikki and also scripted by him, broke all box office records in Scotland. As an actor his performances have been acclaimed in stage plays such as *Let Wives Tak Tent* and *A Wee Touch of Class*; in television dramas such as *The Miser, A Winter's Tale* and *Bergerac*; in films such as *The Dollar Bottom, Gorky Park, Local Hero, Comfort and Joy* and *The Girl in the Picture*.

But it is television comedy which has made Rikki Fulton a household name in his beloved Scotland. *Scotch & Wry*, which began in 1978, has broken every audience record. The videos, *Scotch & Wry* and *Double Scotch & Wry*, have broken every BBC video sales record, surpassing such legendary titles as *Monty Python's Flying Circus* and *Fawlty Towers*.

Few subjects are taboo in *Double Scotch & Wry*, which is above all contemporary. It deals with the kind of situations and subjects that are reflected in everyday life. The Rev. I. M. Jolly, Supercop and Dirty Dickie Dandruff are recognisable parodies of characters that Scots see on their television screens or even meet in the street. But the main difference between *Scotch & Wry* and other television comedy shows is that it speaks in an unmistakable Scottish accent.

The Scots are a curious race, apparently obsessed with football, drink and religion. They can even joke about death. They seem to be hopelessly divided: Glasgow and Edinburgh, Highlands and Lowlands, Protestants and Catholics. But they have one thing in common: a dislike of the auld enemy, England. Of course, much of it has to do with living up to an image that is expected of them. In reality the Scots prefer curries and fish suppers to haggis and porridge. They wear jeans and trainers rather than kilts and brogues. They live in towns and tenements rather than glens and but-and-bens. The English should worry! The only thing that they are missing is *Scotch & Wry*, which the Scots are cannily keeping to themselves. That is why there is so much laughter in Scottish homes at Hogmanay.

*Gordon Menzies*

# SUPERCOP

•

## SUPERCOP AND TAGGART

### *by Bob Black*

SUPERCOP Rikki Fulton; TAGGART Mark McManus

*A typical street corner on a gloomy evening. A car is parked at the kerb on double yellow lines near a 'No Parking' sign. Along comes Supercop. He dismounts from his bike, undoes his goggles, which fly over his head behind him, approaches the car and slaps his gloves down on the bonnet.*

SUPERCOP Okay, Stirling, oot the car! I said oot the car, pal. Fast!

*The door opens and out of the car steps Taggart. He makes to speak, but Supercop won't let him. Supercop is at his most officious, superior and bumptious!*

SUPERCOP No, no! Don't speak, pal! Don't say a word! You're in enough bother as it is. I mean, I cannae count . . . I cannae COUNT the number of bye-laws and road traffic regulations that you've violated. So just keep your mouth shut.

TAGGART No, but listen –

SUPERCOP (*firmer, more threatening*) Naw, you listen! This is the police you're dealing with! (*Pointing to his helmet*) This doesn't say

'kiss-me-quick' y'know! This says 'Police'. You're already in trouble. All we have to ascertain is how MUCH trouble. (*He has taken out his pencil and notebook, and Taggart is looking at him very coldly*) So . . . name!

TAGGART  Taggart!

SUPERCOP  Taggart . . . (*writing it down*) First name?

TAGGART  Chief Inspector!

SUPERCOP  (*makes to write, then stops*) Chief . . .? Chief In . . .? Inspector? (*Looking at Taggart*) What? Ye mean, like, on the buses?

TAGGART  Not on the buses, ye dunderheid! I'm a police officer!

SUPERCOP  (*disbelieving, amused*) Away-yy-yy! Ho-ho, that's the best yet! I mean, I've heard them all! 'I'm a Mason!' or 'I'm pregnant!' or 'I'm a pregnant Mason!' But, a police officer? A wee runt like you? Don't make me laugh! (*He does laugh, mockingly, until Taggart opens his ID wallet and holds it under his nose. Supercop gradually stops laughing and realises the truth*) Aye, well, I suppose I can let ye off wi' a warning this time.

*Taggart grabs Supercop by the lapels, and forces him backwards against the car.*

TAGGART  And I could let you off with suspension and a broken nose!

SUPERCOP  (*greatly alarmed, shaken*) Here, watch it! I'll have you for damaging police property!

TAGGART  There's not a scratch on the car!

SUPERCOP  Stuff your car! Ye've broken my pencil! (*He holds up his pencil for Taggart to see – Taggart gives a sigh of exasperation and lets go of him*) I mean, how was I supposed to know? You don't even look like a policeman. You look more like a Jehovah's Witness.

TAGGART  I'm in plain clothes!

SUPERCOP  Ach, well. Stick in and maybe one day you'll get a nice uniform like mine.

TAGGART  Ye balloon ye! I'm on a case! This is a stake-out!

SUPERCOP  A stake-out? (*looking round*) No much of a place to have a barbecue, is it? Further doon the road there's a wee picnic spot wi –

TAGGART  (*interrupting*) A stake-out, you idiot! I'm watching that building over there! (*He points, then moves closer to Supercop, and speaks confidentially*) I got a tip-off this morning about a suspect. This is his description (*reading from his notebook*): 'Over six feet tall, below average intelligence, with a permanently glaikit look on his face!' (*He looks at Supercop*) Here, it isn't you, is it?

SUPERCOP  (*thinking about it seriously*) No, it cannae be, I'm no' six foot. But listen, if he's in there, why are you out here?

TAGGART  Waiting for back-up.

SUPERCOP  Well the wait's over, pal! Ye've already put my back up. (*Pleased with himself*)

TAGGART  You're right! We can't wait any longer! We'll have to go in and arrest him ourselves! You and me!

SUPERCOP  (*his pleased look vanishing*) You and me? i.e. US . . . together?

TAGGART  Yes! Got a problem?

SUPERCOP  Just one! (*Holding up his pencil*) Have ye got another pencil I could borrow?

11

TAGGART (*grabs Supercop and pulls him face to face, very close*) Forget your bloody pencil! This man's dangerous! We call him the South Side Slasher! (*Spraying him with saliva*)

SUPERCOP (*wiping his face and eyes*) Is that the rain coming on?

TAGGART Are you trying to wind me up?

SUPERCOP (*rattled*) I didnae even know you were clockwork!

TAGGART (*exasperated, pushing him away*) How did you ever get to be a policeman? By writing to *Jim'll Fix It*? We've got to stop this man! He's already slaughtered dozens of innocent people!

SUPERCOP (*realisation dawning very slowly on him*) S-slaughtered? You mean like, slaughtered them dead? (*Uneasy, begins edging away*) Ah, well, slaughtering's no' really in my jurisdiction, I mean, let him try something serious . . . let him go through a red light, and I'll have him! No messin'!!! But s-slaughtering's no' really m-my style. So . . .

TAGGART (*coming over and grabbing him again*) Hold it right there! We've got to do our duty! We can't let him get away with murder!

SUPERCOP Oh no? Sydney Devine's been gettin away wi' it for years!

TAGGART He's got a knife!

SUPERCOP Oh. (*He calms down, and becomes more composed, serious, in control of the situation*) Oh, well, say no more! I'm your man! (*Starts walking towards the corner*) In that case I'll go in there myself! I'll hunt him down! I'll corner him! I'll face him and his knife!

TAGGART And ask him to give himself up?

SUPERCOP (*looking back*) No! (*Holding up his pencil*) Ask him to sharpen my pencil!

*Taggart is exasperated! Supercop turns to go on his way.*

# SUPERCOP AND THE GETAWAY CAR

## *by Colin Bostock-Smith*

SUPERCOP Rikki Fulton; DRIVER Gregor Fisher; SECOND
CROOK Finlay Welsh; THIRD CROOK/RADIO VOICE Tony Roper;
FOURTH CROOK John Casey

*The usual setting, with Supercop pulling up in front of a white Citroën
car. In the white car are four very obvious criminals. One of them
even has a stocking over his head. Supercop gets off his bike, undoes
his goggles and walks up to the driver's window.*

DRIVER (*fatalistic, pushing his hands through the open window in
order to be handcuffed*) All right, all right . . .

SUPERCOP That one, it's a peanut that doesn't melt in your hand.
(*Taking one of the outstretched hands and shaking it*)

DRIVER Look, we give up. Let's get on with it, shall we?

SUPERCOP Get on whit what?

DRIVER Well . . . taking us down the police station.

SUPERCOP Ah, you want to get to the police station, do you? Oh, I
can get you there all right.

DRIVER Yes, of course you can.

SUPERCOP (*straightening*) Of course I can. I'm a polisman. I work
there. Now, go down here, take the first right, then go on to the
crossing and . . . no, wait a second. Not the first crossing . . .

DRIVER (*beginning to realise*) Er . . . officer, why did you pull us in?

SUPERCOP (*bending down again*) I didnae pull you in. I always
stop here, to radio headquarters.

SECOND CROOK Then you don't know about the rob . . .

DRIVER (*clamping hand over second crook's mouth*) My friend
means you're not . . . charging us with anything?

SUPERCOP Not unless you want me to. Ha, ha, ha!

DRIVER Ha, ha. Well, we'll be on our way then. Bye . . .

13

SUPERCOP (*stopping him*) Just a moment!

DRIVER What?

SUPERCOP (*indicating third crook*) Why has your friend got a stocking over his head?

DRIVER He . . . he . . . he's got a nasty skin complaint.

SUPERCOP Then I'd better investigate.

DRIVER What? (*alarmed*)

SUPERCOP (*making a joke*) Well – us polis always investigate complaints! Get it? Ha, ha, ha . . .

CRIMINALS (*weakly together*) Ha, ha, ha.

DRIVER Well, we'll be on our way then.

SUPERCOP Just a moment!

DRIVER What?

SUPERCOP I havenae told you how to get to the polis station yet. Tell you what. You follow my bike, and I'll guide you there. No bother.

DRIVER But . . .

SUPERCOP And if you lose me, don't worry about it.

DRIVER I won't.

SUPERCOP I'll put out a call on my radio, if you do, and then one of our patrol cars will pick you up and bring you in.

DRIVER (*ironic, looking at second crook*) Very kind of him.

SUPERCOP Don't mention it. Now . . . aha! Just a second.

*The radio on his bike has started to squawk. He walks towards it, to hear better.*

RADIO VOICE Attention all units. Robbery at Central Bank ten minutes ago. Four suspects escaped in white Citroën getaway car. Keep constant watch on all routes. Do not approach, these men are dangerous. Urgent . . .

*Supercop goes back to the car. Again the driver puts his hands out of the window, as before.*

DRIVER (*fatalistic*) All right, all right, I know . . .

SUPERCOP (*taking his hand and shaking it again*) Aye. I'm sorry.

14

DRIVER (*bitter*) YOU'RE sorry!

SUPERCOP Aye – I cannae take you to the polis station.

DRIVER Oh . . . oh, really?

SUPERCOP You heard Headquarters. I have to stay and watch for this white car full of suspicious men. But listen, you take the first right, go down to the crossing and get someone there to direct you to the polis station. By the way, you'd better watch that money – you might get it stole. There are some funny folk about. Some of them have got stockings over their heads – but they haven't got dermatitis like you. Keep an eye out for the car, will you? Okay?

DRIVER Fine . . . fine . . . thanks . . . bye.

*He drives off.*

SUPERCOP Goodbye, sir . . . (*He watches the car go, and his expression changes to disappointment*) Oh my God, come back, come back! There! I knew it! He's gone the wrong way already.

# SUPERCOP AND THE UNDERTAKERS

## *by Colin Gilbert*

JIM Pat Doyle; HARRY Gregor Fisher; SUPERCOP Rikki Fulton;
WOMAN Miriam Margolyes

*A hearse is stuck in the snow. Two undertakers in the hearse, both in high spirits and very much the worse for drink. The driver is revving the engine, trying to get the hearse moving again. Both find the situation highly amusing and a bottle of whisky is being passed back and forth.*

JIM (*the driver*) Jeez Harry, I think we're stuck in . . . stuck, ha, ha, ha, ha.

HARRY (*getting out*) No problem Jim, I'll dig us out . . . burrrrrrppppp! (*Starts to sing*) I'm getting buried in the morning.

*As he sings the above refrain, he staggers and slithers round to the back door of the hearse, opens it, takes out a spade and starts to dig around the rear wheel of the vehicle, falling, singing and slithering as he does so. Supercop enters on his bike and comes to a halt. As he surveys the scene he undoes his goggles. Harry looks up and sees him.*

HARRY (*ebullient*) Happy New Year to both of youse.

SUPERCOP (*walking over to him*) Happy New Year, Mr Burke or Mr Hare, you can't do that.

HARRY Can't do what?

SUPERCOP (*indicating spade*) You can't bury dead bodies in the middle of the ring road.

HARRY (*in drunken incomprehension*) What are you talking about?

SUPERCOP New to this game, are you? Well, there are places called cemeteries which . . .

HARRY No, you silly constable, I'm not burying anybody. Burrrpppp. We just took a wrong turning and now we're buried in the snow.

16

SUPERCOP (*eyeing the devastation*) A wrong turning . . . you're half-way up a lamp post and you say you took a wrong turning.

HARRY (*clambering up Supercop's jacket*) Brp!

SUPERCOP Wait a minute.

HARRY Aye?

SUPERCOP Have you been drinking?

HARRY What makes you think that ossifer?

SUPERCOP (*with a self-satisfied smile*) Well, when you've been a guardian of the law for as long as I have, you start to notice the little things, things that only a real professional would think important.

HARRY Like what?

SUPERCOP Well, like, for instance, your pupils. I know you can't see them but they're there. They're more dilated than usual, the veins in your face are suffused with blood and then, of course, there's the real clincher.

HARRY What's that?

SUPERCOP You've been sick on my boots.

HARRY (*shouting to his colleague*) Hey Jim, the polis here thinks we've been drinking.

JIM (*coming round side of hearse, pouring whisky into pint mug*) We haven't been drinking, officer, we're still drinking . . . here, have one yourself.

SUPERCOP No, no, no, I couldn't.

HARRY Ach come on, it's Hogmanay.

SUPERCOP (*a bit more uncertain*) Look, you don't understand, I'm on duty.

JIM Well that's all right, this stuff's duty-free.

SUPERCOP Duty-free?

JIM Aye.

SUPERCOP Well I suppose that makes it OK, and it is New Year after all. Just a wee one then.

   *Jim hands him the full pint mug.*

JIM Good on you. Happy New Year.

**SUPERCOP** Happy New Year boys. (*Taking a couple of good slugs*) Brrrpppppp. (*Looking at glass*) Very nice. It's not much fun for any of us to be working New Year's Eve.

**HARRY** Aye, we're no working. We're going to a party at the crematorium.

**SUPERCOP** A party? Oh I love parties. Nobody's asked me to a party this year. (*Getting a bit maudlin*) Nobody ever asks me to parties any more.

**JIM** Well, why don't you come with us to the crematorium?

**HARRY** Aye, you'll love it, plenty of booze, plenty of women and a lovely big roaring fire.

*We hear bells.*

**SUPERCOP** Oh, hey, that's the bells.

**ALL** Happy New Year.

*They hold hands and start to sing 'Auld lang syne'. Supercop is standing next to the coffin. As they sing, the lid opens, a woman sits up, grabs Supercop's hand and joins in the singing. Supercop does a double-take and turns to Harry.*

**SUPERCOP** Er, excuse me, excuse me, your dead body's singing.

**JIM** That's amazing, she couldn't sing before.

*Harry stops singing, Jim stops singing, and corpse continues.*

18

# SUPERCOP AND THE PRIEST

## *by Colin Bostock-Smith*

SUPERCOP Rikki Fulton; PRIEST Tony Roper

*The main street. Supercop pulls up a car, gets off his bike and saunters up to the car, undoing his goggles.*

SUPERCOP (*not looking in the window*) OK Stirling. Cor! Eighty miles an hour down the High Street, the wrong way round the War Memorial, and then straight across my path, nearly killing me. Oot of the car, you're in big trouble, my son!

PRIEST (*as he now reveals himself to be*) Am I, my son?

SUPERCOP (*realising*) Oh, sorry, Father Brendan. It's you. But really, you ought to know better. You nearly killed me.

PRIEST I trust you will forgive me, my son.

SUPERCOP Sorry, Father, but I can't. The law must take its course. Now then . . . (*getting out his notebook*) Name . . .

PRIEST Have I seen you at mass recently, my son?

SUPERCOP Oh, ah, well, actually, no, Father.

PRIEST Or confession?

SUPERCOP Oh . . . no.

PRIEST So if I had killed you just now, you would have gone to judgement a sinner!

SUPERCOP Well . . . aye . . .

PRIEST Without my knowledge, I would have sent a soul to everlasting retribution. Oh, what a terrible burden you would have placed on me!

SUPERCOP Oh . . . I never thought of it like that.

PRIEST No, you wouldn't! You just wander around not in a state of grace, putting yourself in the way of innocent people, who might then send you to purgatory! How could you, my son? How could you?

SUPERCOP I'm . . . I'm terribly sorry, Father.

PRIEST (*slightly mollified*) Aye. Well, don't let it happen again. (*getting into car*)

SUPERCOP Oh, I won't, Father, I promise, I won't.

PRIEST We'll say no more about it – a blessing on you, then, my son. Goodnight.

SUPERCOP Aye, the same to you. Goodnight, Father.

*The priest drives off.*

SUPERCOP Ah, he's a hard man, that Father. And thank heavens he doesn't know I'm a Protestant.

# SUPERCOP AND THE POPE

## *by Laurie Rowley*

SUPERCOP Rikki Fulton; CHAUFFEUR Tony Roper;
THE POPE Extra

*The Pope, surrounded by a plastic partition, stands on the Popemobile, a white convertible with the top down and an elevated platform on the back seat. The vehicle has broken down and the chauffeur is trying to get it started. Supercop stops, undoes his goggles, then approaches the car. He has his own ideas as to what this vehicle is. Looking up at the Pope, he stands with legs apart and hand on hips.*

SUPERCOP I'm sorry pal, you can't sell hot dogs around here . . . (*no response from the Pope*) . . . oh I see, refusing to talk without a solicitor, eh?

*Supercop slaps his gloves on the bonnet and talks to the chauffeur.*

Okay Stirling – out of the car.

*The chauffeur steps out.*

CHAUFFEUR (*in an Italian accent*) What ees the matter officer? Anything wrong?

20

SUPERCOP I'll ask the questions, Giuseppe. I'm the law and you're the suspect. Got that?

CHAUFFEUR Suspect? What suspect? I haven't done anything wrong!

SUPERCOP That's what Al Capone said, son – only he had a better accent than you. (*Getting out his notebook*) Right, name?

CHAUFFEUR Andrea Bartolo Carlo Dionosettie Emelio Fettuccinni.

SUPERCOP Oh, you're from Largs. Now, I must warn you that anything you say may be taken down and used in evidence.

CHAUFFEUR Porca misseria, ayoota mi. Madre mia, da questo stupido Scotscese.

SUPERCOP (*closing the notebook*) Aye well, I only said MAY be taken down, didn't I? Now, can I have a perusal of your Hot Dog Vendor's Licence?

CHAUFFEUR We're not selling any hot dogs.

SUPERCOP I'm not surprised round here. You want to be at Ibrox today. The crowd would go daft.

CHAUFFEUR No, no, we're on our way to the airport. We come from America, via Scotland and then to Italy.

SUPERCOP Oh, yer wi' Kwik Travel?

CHAUFFEUR No, no. The engine she conka oota.

SUPERCOP Oh, come on pal you're not talking to Chief Inspector Taggart now you know.

CHAUFFEUR You no' understand. We're incognito.

SUPERCOP Naw, we're no'. We're in Cardonald.

CHAUFFEUR You're making a terrible mistake – don't you know who this is?

*The Pope is holding a single rose. Supercop stares at him and a look of recognition gradually dawns.*

SUPERCOP It's no'. Is it him? Is it? No! I often wondered what happened to Sydney Devine.

CHAUFFEUR Forgive him, Holiness, he's just an atheist.

SUPERCOP I'm not an atheist. For your information pal I've got religion. I'm a born-again Grousellarian, so there!

CHAUFFEUR What's that?

SUPERCOP Oh the Grousellarian movement's very popular in Glasgow. Yes, we believe that after death we go to a place with no licensing laws and Scotland win the World Cup every four years.

CHAUFFEUR Is that your idea of heaven?

SUPERCOP Can you think of a better idea? Anyway, pal, I'm afraid I can't let you stay here.

CHAUFFEUR I already tell you, the engine she conka oota but don't worry, I used the telephone and we're waiting for a mechanic.

SUPERCOP You're waiting for a mechanic? On New Year's Day? In Glasgow? In Cardonald? Ha, ha, I hope you've got sleeping bags in that car, son, you wouldnae get anyone out today, not even if it was the Pope himself.

CHAUFFEUR So what can I do? The engine won't start. Listen . . . (*puts his arm through the open window and turns the ignition, but the engine just coughs once and dies*)

SUPERCOP Okay son, we'll have to push it into that side street out of the way. (*Whistles to the Pope*) Come on and get down, Jimmy, and give us a hand, will you?

CHAUFFEUR Hey, what are you saying? That's no way to speak to him?

SUPERCOP Right enough, he'd get his frock all mucky.

*We hear the strains of a marching band.*

SUPERCOP Wait a minute, listen. Oh it's too late, here they come . . .

CHAUFFEUR Who?

SUPERCOP The Orange Walk . . .(*the Pope frowns slightly*)

*The noise of the band is getting louder. The chauffeur begins to panic.*

CHAUFFEUR Orange Walk? Madre Mia. We've got to get him out of there.

*The Pope is praying and looking up to Heaven.*

SUPERCOP Take it from me pal, you're going to need a miracle.

*Pope flies out the Popemobile heavenwards. Supercop and the chauffeur are dumbfounded.*

# SUPERCOP AND DR CRIPPEN

## by Laurie Rowley

SUPERCOP Rikki Fulton; DR CRIPPEN Gregor Fisher;
BODY Judy Sweeney

*At night. Supercop dismounts from his motorbike and approaches a
car, undoing his goggles. On the roof rack there is a naked corpse
under a tarpaulin. Her right leg has slipped and is dangling over the
rear passenger door. Supercop takes off his gloves and taps on the
driver's window.*

SUPERCOP  Okay, Stirling . . . out of the car.

> *The driver gets out. He is wearing a raincoat buttoned up to his
> throat and rimless specs. His hair is parted in the middle. Supercop
> is startled momentarily by his sinister appearance.*

DOCTOR  (*stuffing corpse's leg back under the tarpaulin*) Wha-what
have I done, officer?

SUPERCOP  What have ye done? Give us credit for havin' some
powers of observation. You KNOW what you've done . . . and what's
more you know that AH know what you've done.

DOCTOR  All right, all right, I confess . . . I confess . . . I'll tell you
everything.

SUPERCOP  That's better. When did you first notice that you had a
faulty rear indicator light? (*Supercop and Dr Crippen carry on at
cross purposes, regardless of each other*)

DOCTOR  It all began on our honeymoon . . . that's when she started
to nag me . . .

SUPERCOP  . . . which is in direct contravention of the traffic
regulations.

DOCTOR  She kept on at me to come to bed, when all I wanted to do
was watch *Take the High Road.*

SUPERCOP  And ye wernae even using hand signals . . .

DOCTOR  After the honeymoon it got worse . . . (*arm slips from
under tarpaulin*)

SUPERCOP Naw, it's too late tae use hand signals NOW, pal. Ye shoulda thoughta that before. Here, yer girlfriend wants tae put on simmit – she's freezin' cauld.

DOCTOR For seventeen months she never stopped nagging me. It was driving me insane.

SUPERCOP Aye, and talkin' about drivin' . . . you are a menace tae other road users, pal. You've really put your foot in it this time (*foot comes down*) . . . and so's yer passenger. Here, do ye mind? Ah'm trying tae make out a report here.

*As he puts the leg back, the arm slips out. This happens again. The Doctor rambles on.*

DOCTOR . . . then tonight I finally snapped. I waited till she'd stopped talking which meant she was fast asleep, then I covered her face with a pillow . . . I murdered her until she was dead . . . just like I did with all my other wives . . . he, he . . . he, he . . .

SUPERCOP What has she been drinking? A good few stiff ones, I'll bet. A good few stiff ones . . . Please yoursel' . . . Right, pal, we'll have a squint at your documents.

DOCTOR (*coming out of his trance*) I beg your pardon?

SUPERCOP Documents . . . bumph . . . driving licence . . . insurance . . . MOT certificate . . . bingo cards . . .

DOCTOR Oh . . . I'm afraid I don't carry any documents on my person, officer.

SUPERCOP In that case we'll require a few particulars. Name?

DOCTOR Crippen . . .

SUPERCOP (*writing*) Cripp . . . en.

DOCTOR Doctor . . . Crippen.

SUPERCOP Aw . . . you're a doctor, are you?

DOCTOR That's right.

SUPERCOP Listen, doctor, ah've had this currybunkle on the back of my neck . . . here, wait a minute . . . you're not the same Doctor Crippen I've seen in Madame Tussaud's Chamber of Horrors, ur ye??? The one that done in all his wives . . .

DOCTOR (*modestly*) My grandfather.

SUPERCOP Get away. No kiddin'? He's ma favourite! I've always thought that if ma missus had met up wi' Dr Crippen before her and me started winchin' I would be a happy man today. Here, gonnae give us yer autograph?

*Supercop hands notebook to the doctor.*

DOCTOR Certainly. (*Writing*)

SUPERCOP Ah tell ye what, Doctor. Just ye bring yer documents roon tae the station the morra and we'll forget aw aboot it.

DOCTOR Thank you, officer.

SUPERCOP Not at all – thank YOU.

*They shake hands and the doctor goes to the driver's door. The hand slips out of the tarpaulin and Supercop shakes it.*

SUPERCOP Heh . . . WAIT A MINUTE. D'you think I'm stupit? YOU thought I didnae notice, didn't ye? You thought ye'd got away wi' it, didn't ye?

*The doctor offers his wrists for handcuffing. Supercop snatches the book from his hand.*

SUPERCOP Nearly away with my notebook there!

# TRADES AND PROFESSIONS

•

## THE GALLOWGATE GOURMET

*by Robert Sykes Andrews*

DIRTY DICKY DANDRUFF Rikki Fulton

*Café kitchen set up for TV cookery programme, showing title on screen: 'More Recipes from Dick's Delicat'messen'. Dirty Dicky stands behind a table in a large kitchen. The kitchen is filthy, with dirt and food stains on the walls and grime-encrusted kitchenware lying all over the place. He is unashamed and looks unwashed. His white chef's jacket and hat are covered in stains and there is a lighted cigarette dangling from the corner of his mouth.*

DICKY Hallawrerr, housewives. And welcome once again to the kitchen of my Motorway Caff for another gander at how to cook up meals just like the ones that we serve to our clientèle. And though I say it myself, I can cook up meals better than most. Now this week I'm goin' to show you how to prepare one of my unique home-made pies – or as they're known on the M1, my foot-and-mouth specials. And our first requirement is one bakin' bowl.

*He produces a large, dirty baking bowl with cracks in it and a sheep's head. He takes out the sheep's head.*

We left the eyes in to see us through the week. Into which I have beforehand bunged a half-pound of flour, a cupfu' of water an' a

27

dawd of butter. We now give the mixture a bit of a knead and by Jove it needs it. And just let me digress here to say that I've had a couple of letters complainin' aboot me no washin' my hands before I work with edible foodstuffs. An' all right, fair's fair, a bit of hygiene never hurt anybody. So before we came on the air I gave the offending appendages a guid scrub wae soap an' water. And I washed my hands as well!

*He laughs uproariously at his own joke.*

Now then . . .

*He wipes his nose with the back of his hand, then sticks his hands into the bowl and begins kneading the mixture.*

. . . work the mixture aboot until it turns intae a paste that you dump on a baking board an' roll intae pastry. Earlier I had my assistant chef Clarty Claude make up some pastry for me.

*He shouts to someone on the other side of the kitchen.*

Hae Claude, see us that pastry!

*A rough square of cooked pastry is thrown from the other side of the kitchen. Dicky tries to catch it but it goes flying past and lands in a sink full of dirty dishes soaking in water.*

Gaun, ya big mug, ye.

*He goes over to the sink, pulls the rather rubbery-looking pastry out of the water and wrings it out. Just then, he notices something in the sink.*

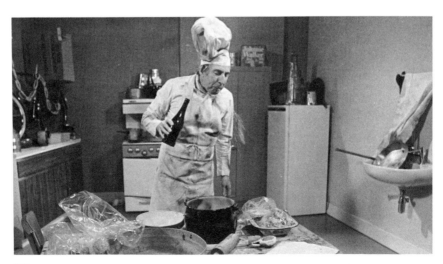

Hey Clarty, how many times have I told you aboot pitting your dirty underwear in wae the dinner dishes? You'll ruin the elastic.

*He walks back to the table and flings the Y-fronts on to the table.*

These might come in handy later. Now pit the pastry into the baking bowl.

*He lays the pastry in the dirty baking bowl.*

An' we're ready for the pie fillin'. Now, through the years, many a connoisseur of the culinary arts has come tae me an' enquired as to just what I put intae my pies. In fact only the other day two men came round after hearin' numerous reports of their distinctive flavour an' almost demanded to be informed of the ingredients. But the fact that they were from the Sanitary didnae impress me at all; and I told them to 'phone me about it. So let's go to the café freezer to get our ingredients.

*He walks over to a large freezer but on the way over he trips. He looks down at the floor and tramps on something with his foot.*

Thae bloody big cockroaches would trip you up as soon as look at you.

*He opens the lid of the freezer and looks inside.*

Let's see noo.

*He peers into the freezer, gives a few loud coughs, then sticks his hand down inside and pulls out a leg of mutton, which he puts on top of the freezer. He sticks his hand back down inside and pulls out a dead cat by the tail. Suddenly he realises that it can be seen by the camera and he quickly shoves it back. Then he sticks his hand down inside the freezer again.*

An', oh aye, here's the ideal scrumptious fillin' for a pie. A few leftovers – picked up by old Jessie the cleaner. Well, waste not, want not.

*He pulls a small, dirty, battered tin bucket out of the freezer, and goes back over to the table, stamping on another cockroach, which he puts in the pail with a loud clang.*

Oh well it's protein.

*He pours the vile-looking contents of the bucket into the baking tin, hitting the bucket with his hand to get it all out, and lifts the wine bottle.*

Add a little white wine.

*He swallows some and spits the remainder into the pie.*

That's about the quantity – a mouthful and a half.

*He puts his hand in the tin and pulls out a bun that has a set of dentures clamped on to it in a vice-like grip.*

Clarty, I keep tellin' you, you're makin' thae rock buns too hard. Now all we have to do is cover it with some more pastry.

*He crimps the pastry with the dentures.*

Then shove the pie intae the oven on a low heat for aboot two hours, or until it explodes.

*He picks up the underpants. Then he goes over to the oven, opens the door and pulls out a repulsive-looking pie with a sheep's head on the top and what looks like black slime oozing out of it. He sits it on the table.*

Like all good TV cooks, of course, I have one already cooking. And the final result is this mouthwaterin' delicacy, guaranteed to put hairs on your chest, and make you run faster than the Bionic Woman.

Well that's all for this week folks. Look in again next week when I'll be baking the humble Scots salmon and turning it into an Italian treat call Salmonella. So, bon appétit.

*Music: 'Something's cooking in the kitchen'.*

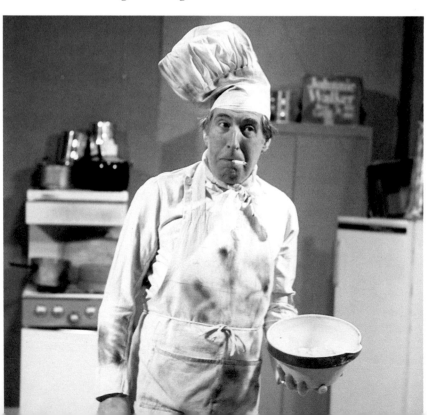

# DEAD CHUFFED

## *by Bob Black*

DOUGALD Gregor Fisher; MUM Juliet Cadzow;
SHUGHIE Rikki Fulton

*A sign on a wall says: 'S. W. DUFF, Funeral Directors'. Underneath it, there is a Christmassy sign with tinsel borders, saying: 'A Happy New Year to all our customers'. We find ourselves in a small, drab funeral parlour, with various coffins on display. A bell tinkles, the door opens, and Dougald comes in. He is a dutiful son, carefully leading his mum, an elderly, sour-faced, cheerless, disapproving, severe, 'wee free kirk' type of woman.*

DOUGALD  This way, Mammy. This way.

MUM  (*severe*) Och, Dougald! Stop fussing! Go and get some service.

*Shughie has crept up behind them.*

SHUGHIE  Boo!

*Shughie appears. He is wearing a very loud suit with a dazzling shirt, tie and socks! He is very cheery, cheeky and confident – not at all the usual sort of undertaker.*

SHUGHIE  Hullo! Season's greetings an' that!

DOUGALD  (*taken aback*) Oh, er, are you the . . , undertaker?

SHUGHIE  That I am! S. W. Duff, at your service! 'Go with Duff! You'll be DEAD Chuffed!' Shughie Duff, that's me! The man who put the FUN in Funeral, and, if I say so mysel', the crème de la crematorium. What can I do for you?

DOUGALD  Well, I . . . I've lost my father.

SHUGHIE  He didnae come in here, sir! There's been no one in all day!

DOUGALD  No, I don't mean that . . . I mean he's . . . deceased.

SHUGHIE  Oh, you mean – he's deid! And you want to make some . . . (*more delicately*) . . . arrangements?

DOUGALD  Yes, but . . . (*very unsure*) perhaps I should go somewhere else. I'm not too happy with your decorum.

SHUGHIE (*looking round*) Neither am I, sir. In fact, I plan to have the whole place emulsioned as soon as possible.

DOUGALD No, I mean . . . your manner. Your attitude.

SHUGHIE Look, sir, I don't do things the old-fashioned way. All that greetin' and cryin' and everyone sitting round wi' their faces trippin' them! It's worse than *The Hogmanay Show*. I like to see off our dearly departed with a smile and a laugh! It's how they'd want it, sir.

DOUGALD (*almost convinced*) Perhaps you're right.

SHUGHIE (*going behind the counter*) So if I could take a few details . . . Now, about the service. Is it smoking or non-smoking?

DOUGALD (*surprised*) What?

SHUGHIE (*amused at himself*) Oh, sorry, sir. I mean cremation or burial?

DOUGALD I don't know. (*Looking round*) What do you think, Mammy?

SHUGHIE (*surprised*) Oh, is this your mother, sir? Forgive me. I thought you'd been followed in by some old wino! (*He crosses the parlour to shake hands with Mum*) Madam, may I extend my deepest sympathy. Your husband must have been a fine man.

MUM (*frosty*) He was a loathsome blasphemous toad!

SHUGHIE Good for you, hen! I'm glad you havenae let yoursel' be overcome wi' grief!

MUM (*severe*) He sinned! He drank! He fell among loose women and indulged in pleasures of the flesh! He will find no salvation now he has passed on!

SHUGHIE (*shrugs*) Maybe no'. But it sounds as if he had a helluva good time while he was here! (*He looks at Dougald*) Your father drank?

DOUGALD He was practically an alcoholic.

SHUGHIE (*making notes*) We'd better forget the cremation, then. We'd never get the flame oot! (*looking up*) So it's just your straight-forward burial, I suppose?

DOUGALD (*his doubts are returning*) I think so. But . . . have you had much experience?

SHUGHIE Tons! Tons of experience. I've popped more folk into tiny wee boxes than Barratt Homes!

DOUGALD It's just that, forgive me, but you're not how I pictured an undertaker.

SHUGHIE Well, see, when I left school I thought ahead. I planned my career. I thought, 'What are folk doin' now that they'll still be doin' a hundred years frae now!? What does EVERYBODY do? Every man and woman! Rich or poor! What do we ALL have to do, eventually?' And of course, the answer came to me . . .

DOUGALD And you became an undertaker?

SHUGHIE No, I went to work for Shanks of Barrhead! But I got piss. . . . er . . . fed up wi' that job, so I went into this game! Believe me, sir, your father is in excellent hands.

*Shughie comes out from behind the counter, and moves to the first coffin in the display area.*

SHUGHIE Now, I can do you our 'Restive Festive Service' . . .

DOUGALD What's that?

SHUGHIE (*indicating the first coffin*) That's a plain coffin, but we wrap it in Christmas paper and tinsel.

DOUGALD (*not keen at all*) I don't think so . . .

SHUGHIE (*moving on to the second coffin*) Well then, there's our 'Basic Bargain Burial'. That comes wi' green shield stamps, a free decanter and a voucher for ten pounds off your next purchase . . . (*looks over towards Mum*) which might be sooner than ye think.

MUM (*she suddenly shouts over*) I want him buried quickly!

*Shughie suddenly has an idea. He snaps his fingers and turns away from the coffins.*

SHUGHIE  I wonder if I could suggest our 'Ratchet Casket'?

DOUGALD  What's that?

SHUGHIE  (*enthusiastically demonstrating*) My own design! A pointed coffin wi' a thread on it, and ye sort of SCREW the deceased intae the ground! It's a great savin' on time and space!

DOUGALD  (*shocked*) That's disgusting.

SHUGHIE  How is it? I buried eighteen folk that way last month and didnae hear a word of complaint frae wan o' them!

DOUGALD  (*growing irate*) Your ideas are . . . are sick! Each one's worse than the last! My father was a decent man! He had his pride! He was in the Navy!

SHUGHIE  (*perking up – another idea*) Oh! Oh, well, in that case, sir, might I suggest a burial at sea?

DOUGALD  (*suspicious*) Is . . . is it proper and decent?

SHUGHIE  (*very honest and sincere – almost holy*) Trust me, sir. We do a 'Service at Sea' that is very tasteful, very respectful. And above all . . . (*rather moved*) . . . very, very dignified.

DOUGALD  (*pleased*) Oh, well, that's what we'll have! If it isn't too expensive!

SHUGHIE  Expensive? Not at all sir. (*He has moved to the third coffin now – the one lying flat on the trestle table*) In fact, the dearest bit is fixing the outboard motor to the coffin!

*Shughie moves away the coffin lid to reveal a very powerful outboard motor attached to the end of the coffin!*

# SANTA SURGERY

## *by Bob Black*

DOCTOR Tony Roper; NURSE Judy Sweeney; SANTA Rikki Fulton

*A doctor's surgery. The doctor is sitting behind his desk, writing some notes. A nurse is at the filing cabinet nearby. The doctor is smart, well groomed and well spoken.*

DOCTOR  Right, Nurse. Send the next one in please.

NURSE  Yes, Doctor.

*She goes to the door, opens it and looks out.*

NURSE  The Doctor will see you now.

*Enter Santa Claus in the traditional scarlet suit, with a big beard and a large sack over his shoulder. But he is a coarse, rude, ill-tempered Santa.*

SANTA  I should bloody well think so, too! What's the game, eh? What's the game? Keepin' a man o' my age waitin'! I'm 687 years old, you know! Next birthday!

NURSE  (*taken aback*) I . . . I'm sorry.

SANTA Aye . . . well . . . I'll let you off just this once, I suppose.
Seein' as you're such a wee cracker! (*He slaps her bottom as she
turns to go*) You can hang your stockin's on the end of my bed any
day, hen!

*The nurse goes out, embarrassed and very indignant. Santa glares at
the doctor.*

SANTA But as for you! Dr Doolittle! Or to be mair precise, Dr Do-
Absolutely-Sod-All!

*The doctor looks up from his notes now, very surprised.*

DOCTOR Goodness me! I'm sorry, I didn't realise! I mean, no one
told me it was you . . .

*He gets up and comes round the desk.*

SANTA Well of course it's me! And I've got better things to do than
hang aboot this place all day! I've got Carol Singers waitin' for me
back home!

DOCTOR Carol Singers?

SANTA Aye! And a wee stoatir she is, too!

DOCTOR I see. But what brings you here. Mr, er, Father, er, Santa?
Have you a problem?

36

SANTA  I have! And I suspect severe exhaustion, and flu.

DOCTOR  And what makes you think that?

SANTA  'Cos I've just flu all the way frae the North Pole and I'm severely knackered! ! (*Growing angry*) Do you know, three times I've phoned this midden! Three times! And each time I was telt you don't make house calls!

DOCTOR  That's quite correct. I don't make house calls. Still, seeing as you're here, how can I help?

SANTA  (*seating himself*) Well, the fact of the matter is, I want a line aff work.

DOCTOR  (*surprised*) Pardon?

SANTA  I want to sign on the panel. Two days'll do. Three would be better. From Christmas Eve until Boxing Day.

DOCTOR  But why?

SANTA  To be perfectly honest, I'm pig-sick of workin' over Christmas.

DOCTOR  What!?

SANTA  By the time I get home I'm that shagged-out, all I do is put my feet up and fall asleep! It's terrible! I miss all the specials on the telly, so I do. I'm the only man in the world who's never seen *The Great Escape*! That's how bad it is!

DOCTOR  But surely you get a lot of job satisfaction? Winging lightly across the sky, sleigh bells jingling. It's very romantic.

SANTA  Romantic!? Have YOU ever sat behind half a dozen reindeer for any length of time? It's no laughing matter, pal! Especially when the wind's against you. You cannae hear the sleigh bells for the noise. To say nothin' of the revoltin' view I'm stuck wi' for mile after mile! And for what? A glass of lukewarm milk and a soddin' biscuit!

DOCTOR  But everybody loves you.

SANTA  Away ye go! Oh, aye, for a week maybe, or ten days, it's all 'Santa I want a transformer' and 'Santa I want My Little Pony'. They can have my bloody reindeer if they like. Then, come Boxing Day, it's 'Sod off Santa!' 'Don't call us we'll call you!' Well, no' this year, China, I want a break!

*The doctor looks very serious, dignified and officious.*

DOCTOR  Well I'm afraid I can't give you one now. I'm sorry, but you're traditional. You've got a serious duty to perform, just like me. And you shouldn't try to wriggle out of it.

37

SANTA (*abashed*) I suppose you're right, Doctor. It was too much to hope for.

*He stands to go.*

DOCTOR If you've any real problems, come and see me, but remember I don't make house calls. (*Writing in his notepad now*) Before you go, though, I want to give you this . . .

*He tears off the page and hands it to Santa.*

SANTA What is it? A prescription?

DOCTOR No. My Christmas list.

SANTA Oh. (*reads from the list*) 'Golf clubs, Trivial Pursuit, soap-on-a-rope, and Y-fronts.' Okay, Doc, I'll arrange that for you. (*Swings his sack on to his shoulder*) And I'll expect you at the North Pole on Christmas morning to collect them.

DOCTOR (*surprised*) To collect them!?

SANTA Aye! See, frae now on, I don't do house calls! Just like you! !

*Exit Santa with a ho-ho-ho!*

# THE CHEMIST SHOP

## by *John A. Stewart*

CHEMIST Rikki Fulton; MAN Gregor Fisher

*A chemist shop. A man enters, wearing a top hat and a morning suit. He is obviously on his way to a wedding.*

CHEMIST Can I help you sir?

MAN (*a little hesitant*) Yes, I'm getting married in ten minutes, then I'm dashing straight off to Spain on my honeymoon and er . . . guess what I forgot to get?

CHEMIST (*knowingly*) Say no more, sir, I'm with you. And actually this is your lucky day because erm . . . I've just got some brand-new imported stock. I bet you've never used any like these before sir.

MAN (*interested*) Oh really?

CHEMIST Yes, made in Amsterdam, if you get my drift.

MAN (*eyes lighting up in enthusiasm*) I do, I do.

CHEMIST  A little more expensive than the ordinary ones but . . . ooh la la, c'est magnifique! Are you with me?

MAN  I'm with you, I'm with you.

CHEMIST  Incredibly robust and hard-wearing and yet designed in a revolutionary new way so as to give absolute sensitivity – need I say more, sir?

MAN  (*very excited*) Say no more, say no more.

CHEMIST  But the pièce de résistance is . . .

MAN  Yes, yes?

CHEMIST  You can have any colour you want.

MAN  Oh that's fantastic! What colours have you got?

CHEMIST  (*producing a box of toothbrushes*) Well, you can have a red one or a blue one or a black one . . .

# CHRISTMAS BOX

## *by Niall Clark*

BOYD Gregor Fisher; FIRST DUSTMAN Rikki Fulton;
SECOND DUSTMAN Extra; THIRD DUSTMAN Extra

*A suburban lounge with Christmas decorations. Sitting in his armchair, quite content, reading and eating peanuts is Mr Boyd. The doorbell rings. He gives a sigh of obvious displeasure as he gets out of the chair to answer it. He opens the door. Standing on the step is a dustman.*

BOYD  Yes?

FIRST DUSTMAN  Good evening, sir. I'm your dustman. I've just come to wish you a Merry Christmas.

BOYD  Very kind. Merry Christmas. Goodbye.

*Boyd starts to close the door but the dustman stops him.*

FIRST DUSTMAN  I don't think you quite understand, sir. (*Holding his hand out, obviously for money*) I've come to wish you a VERY MERRY CHRISTMAS INDEED!

BOYD (*shaking the man's hand*) And a VERY MERRY CHRISTMAS to you, too.

*Boyd tries to shut the door but the dustman jams himself in the way and literally shoulders it open again.*

FIRST DUSTMAN Wait a minute, wait a minute, hold on! Is there no' something . . . some wee something . . . that you havenae done?

BOYD (*thinks for a moment*) I havenae wrapped my fish-heids in paper?

FIRST DUSTMAN Your personal habits are of no interest to me, sir! (*Rubbing his thumb and forefinger together*) . . . I was thinking of something more in a financial vein!

BOYD (*the penny drops and he laughs*) Oh, I see! You mean a tip! A gift! A Christmas Box!

FIRST DUSTMAN A Christmas Box!

BOYD No!

FIRST DUSTMAN Whit?!

BOYD I don't believe in giving gratuitous financial donations just because it's Christmas.

*The dustman moves into the room.*

FIRST DUSTMAN You're a hard man, sir. And obviously unfamiliar with the new Union procedure.

BOYD What's that?

FIRST DUSTMAN (*he reaches into his pocket, takes out a little notebook and refers to it*) A detailed record has been kept of all the refuse collected from this house. And in the event of no gratuity being forthcoming . . . (*whistles*) . . . we bring it back!

*Two other dustmen walk in, carrying full bins, which they empty all over Boyd's floor. Piles of grotty rubbish all over the carpet!*

BOYD (*appalled*) Stop! You can't . . .

*The two dustmen leave.*

FIRST DUSTMAN And there's another three hundredweight on the truck!

BOYD (*reaching into his pocket for his wallet*) All right! All right! Anything. Just to stop this madness!

*He slaps a wad of money into the hand of the dustman, who looks pleasantly surprised!*

FIRST DUSTMAN  Oh, well. That's very generous! Thank you. (*Turns to go*) Well, good evening, Mr Hughes.

BOYD  Hughes? My name's Boyd!

FIRST DUSTMAN  (*puzzled*) Boyd? (*He looks for the door number*) Isn't this forty-six?

BOYD  Twenty-six!

FIRST DUSTMAN  (*referring to his notebook*) Twenty-six? Oh, that's different! (*Highly amused, gives Boyd his money back*) Your wife paid this morning. Merry Christmas!

*The dustman walks off cheerfully, leaving Boyd gaping at the rubbish piled on his carpet.*

# JOB CENTRE

## *by Laurie Rowley*

MANAGER Gregor Fisher; BIG CHIEF SWIFT HALF Rikki Fulton

*The manager's office at a typical job centre. The manager sits behind his desk, writing and filling in forms. Then he looks up and calls.*

MANAGER Next!

*The door is flung open and a man bursts in, dressed as a Red Indian medicine man. He is wearing buckskin clothes with fringes, a horned head-dress and war paint. He carries a tomahawk and does a Red Indian war dance. Then he gives an Indian salute.*

BIG CHIEF How! !

MANAGER (*looking up, startled and shocked*) Oh, er, yes . . . y-you'll . . . (*he refers to a list*) You'll be Mr Hodgkinson?

*The Big Chief shakes his head.*

MANAGER Mr Appleby?

*The Big Chief shakes his head.*

MANAGER Big Chief Swift Half?

BIG CHIEF That's the one, Jimmy! That's me!

MANAGER (*still taken aback, gaping*) W-well, come in, Chief, and sit down . . .

*The Big Chief moves, in prancing, war dance steps, to the empty chair in front of the desk. The manager gapes at him.*

BIG CHIEF How! What's the matter, pal? Have you not seen an actual, authentic, genuine medicine man before?

MANAGER Not in Hope Street, no! Eh, which tribe do you actually represent?

BIG CHIEF Me Chief of Semolina tribe!

MANAGER Er, you mean Seminole?

BIG CHIEF No, Semolina! We're a dessert people! (*He laughs, amused*) That's just a little redskin humour I thought I'd throw in . . .

43

MANAGER  Right, Chief, how long have you been out of work exactly?

BIG CHIEF  Since many moon rise over prairie and cast long shadow over great canyon where fish swim in rippling waters.

MANAGER  Pardon?

BIG CHIEF  About two years. (*Rising*) Well if you've got nothing today I'll be on my way . . .

MANAGER  Sit down, Chief, sit down. I'll tell you when to leave.

BIG CHIEF  (*sitting*) Will it take long? I've left my horse Broken Wind on a double brown line.

MANAGER  A double YELLOW line.

BIG CHIEF  He's not called Broken Wind for nothing.

MANAGER  Out of work for two years, eh?

BIG CHIEF  Aye, and I don't mind telling you it excoriates me of all dignity, stigmatises my very being and makes my life a misery. I want a job!

MANAGER  (*looking at a card*) It's okay, Chief, we've found you a job.

BIG CHIEF (*shocked*) Really?

MANAGER Aye, they're wanting a bouncer at the Blue Parrot nightclub.

BIG CHIEF A bouncer at a nightclub? I can't do that!

MANAGER Why not?

BIG CHIEF (*thinking fast*) W-well . . . anyone knows Indians never fight after dark! Surely you know that?

MANAGER To tell you the truth, Chief, I don't think you are a real Indian at all.

BIG CHIEF Not a real Indian? I was born with this head-dress!

MANAGER What did your mother think about that?

BIG CHIEF She was tickled to death!

MANAGER You don't want a job, do you?

BIG CHIEF (*insulted*) Don't want a job? Don't want a job? See here, I've been to every hospital in Glasgow! Is it my fault none of them need a consultant medicine man?

MANAGER No wonder! Is there nothing else you can turn your hand to?

BIG CHIEF Oh, lots of things. I'm very adaptable!

MANAGER So what else can you do?

BIG CHIEF Well . . . I can hunt bears.

MANAGER Away you go! There aren't any bears in Glasgow!

BIG CHIEF You havenae been up Shettleston on a Saturday night, pal.

MANAGER Well, I don't care! I'm sorry, Chief, but if you don't take this nightclub job I'll have to stop your dole!

BIG CHIEF (*getting up*) No! I'm not taking that job. I don't care what you say. (*He turns to go*)

MANAGER They're offering £100 a week, Chief.

BIG CHIEF I'm not interested. (*He turns to go out*)

MANAGER All your meals are thrown in free of charge.

BIG CHIEF (*turning back*) I said I'm not working there and that's final! (*He goes to the door*)

MANAGER And you get to escort the stripper back to her dressing room.

BIG CHIEF When do I start?

*He does a war dance up to the desk, takes the card and exits.*

# BOY MEETS GIRL

•

## BODY LANGUAGE!

*by Bob Black*

TAM Rikki Fulton; WILLIE Tony Roper; FIRST GIRL Annette
Staines; SECOND GIRL Juliet Cadzow; DANCERS Extras

*Tam and Willie are at a hotel disco. They are lounging against a wall, watching the party and feeling slightly bored. Suddenly Willie makes eyes at someone across the room, and then begins to gyrate slightly. He rotates his pelvis in gentle Elvis-like motions. Tam, the older man, notices this. He watches, and a very wary, dubious, suspicious look crosses his face!*

TAM  Whit ye dain'?

WILLIE  (*still gyrating*) Body language!

TAM  (*dubious*) Whit?!

WILLIE  (*still gyrating*) Body language!

TAM  If my body used language like that, I'd wash its mooth oot!

*Willie gyrates throughout the conversation, sometimes embellishing it slightly with shrugs and gestures. He keeps his eyes ahead, as if looking at someone across the room.*

WILLIE  I read a book on it. It's based on primitive tribal instincts and animalistic gestures. It lets ye communicate withoot words. Yur body talks!

TAM  My body a'ready talks! Every time I get home frae work it says, 'I'm knackered!!!'

WILLIE  Try it!

TAM  Away-y-y-y!!

WILLIE  (*still gyrating*) Go on, I'm chattin' up that bird over there! I'm tellin' her, 'My body wants your body!' You chat up her pal!

*Undecided and dubious, Tam looks over.*

TAM  Well . . . ll . . . ll.

*Tam shrugs and reckons he'll give it a try. He watches Willie's gyrations and begins to copy them, but in a rather reserved and inhibited way. Willie's gyrations grow more elaborate. He adds a touch of Shakin' Stevens wobble to the knees. Tam does likewise. After a moment a very attractive girl approaches. She comes towards Willie who keeps gyrating. They start dancing. She kisses him. Tam watches in disbelief. Willie stops gyrating, delighted, and hardly able to believe it himself.*

WILLIE  I've done it! I've done it! I've pulled a bird!!

TAM  Aye? (*wincing and holding his groin*) I think I've pulled a muscle!

WILLIE  Keep at it! Keep at it!

*Tam continues his gyrations with renewed vigour and hope. Encouraged by Willie's success he overdoes the come-on technique. Within moments another beautiful girl approaches Tam. She slaps him hard across the face, and walks off!*

WILLIE  (*shrugs, blasé*) Must've been something you said!

*He walks off with his girl, leaving Tam sprawled out.*

# CHATTING UP

## *by Laurie Rowley*

FRIEND Tony Roper; ALEC Rikki Fulton; GIRL Judy Sweeney

*A bar on board ship – with a disco in progress. Alec, not having much luck with the opposite sex, is getting some advice from a friend.*

FRIEND  . . . look Alec, chatting the birds up is simple. You've just got to use a bit of strategy, that's all . . .

ALEC  Oh, right, I see.

FRIEND  . . . the important thing is to find something you've both got in common, then chat about that, right? And she'll be in your cabin before the night's out, guaranteed.

ALEC  Something in common you say?

FRIEND  Yes, for instance, if she likes Mozart – you like Mozart, if she likes er . . . mince and mushy peas – you like mince and mushy peas, and if she prefers, say Alsatian dogs to wee dogs – then you prefer Alsatian dogs to wee dogs, get it? You must have something in common, right?

ALEC  Right.

FRIEND  (*indicating a girl who is standing alone*) Go on, my son, it never fails.

*Alec approaches the girl. She is stand-offish and smoking.*

ALEC  Hello there.

GIRL  (*quite posh – blowing smoke in his face*) Hello.

ALEC  Fancy coming to my cabin for some mince and mushy peas?

GIRL  I beg your pardon?

*From a distance, Alec's friend is urging him on.*

ALEC  Tell me something, do you like Mozart?

GIRL  Yes I do, as a matter of fact. Do you?

ALEC  I never drink anything else. In fact I've got a bottle in my cabin . . .

GIRL  Look, would you mind leaving me alone? I'm waiting for my boyfriend.

ALEC  Hey, that's a coincidence, so am I . . . (*the girl gives him a strange look*) . . . er well he's not exactly my boyfriend. We have an understanding.

GIRL  Listen here, if you think I'm going to end up in your bed tonight you're completely mistaken – I don't sleep around with men.

ALEC  (*his friend is still urging him on*) Oh I see. Would I be right in assuming you prefer Alsatian dogs?

GIRL  How dare you! (*She starts to walk off*)

ALEC  Hey, wait a minute. Where are you going?

GIRL  If it's any of your concern, I'm going to the ladies room.

ALEC  (*linking arms*) That's a coincidence, so am I.

*The girl grabs a bottle off the bar and breaks it over his head.*

GIRL  (*in a heavy Glasgow accent*) Away and get lost, you bloody pervert!

*She goes. Alec staggers back to his friend.*

FRIEND  Well, did you have anything in common then?

ALEC  Oh aye, I think she's from Glasgow as well.

# UR YE DANCIN'?

## *by John Byrne*

INA Claire Nielson; MINNIE Margo Cunningham;
TOMMY David Hayman; JACKIE Rikki Fulton; DANCERS Extras

*A 1958 dance hall with a glitter ball suspended from the ceiling.
Smoky atmosphere.*

INA  Don't look now but Rock Hudson's gei'in us the eye.

MINNIE  Where?

INA  Ah told ye no' tae look!

*Jackie is eating a fish supper.*

INA  Ower there – wi' the fish supper.

MINNIE  Hus he goat a pal?

INA  Aye, wee guy wi' a big hit fur himsel' . . . keeps winkin' at us.

TOMMY  (*winking*) Gonnae stoap flickin' yer vinegar ett us . . . Gie's
a chip.

JACKIE  Gettaff! You've hud yours! Hing aff . . . Heh, s'em two ower
there dancin'?

*Minnie and Ina are swaying to the music.*

TOMMY  Naw, Ah think it's jist the way they're staunin'. Fancy askin'
them up fur a burl?

JACKIE  Wait'll Ah wipe the grease aff ma hauns. (*He wipes them on
his hair*) Ye goat a comb?

*He combs his hair.*

INA  He's combin' his herr . . . must be serious. Here, is ma face
awright?

MINNIE  Aye, it'll need tae dae . . . it's aw you've got.

INA  Thur comin' ower . . .

TOMMY  Ah still think we should've went tae the Dugs at Shawfield,
Jackie. Ah tellt Ina . . .

JACKIE Aw, can it, Tommy. Her an' Minnie's never gonnae know . . . this is the gemme . . . coupla pints . . . coupla fish suppers, coupla wee ravers . . .

INA S'it ma imagination or his yours goat bandy legs?

MINNIE Is ma froak crumpled? S'ma herr in place?

INA S'oan the tap ae yur heid . . . where else dae ye want it?

TOMMY Ach, c'mon wull gie it a by, Jackie . . . we've still goat time ta catch the last race if we hurry . . . Ina's no' gonnae . . .

JACKIE Furget Ina, Tommy son . . . these two dolls is gei'in us the come hither.

TOMMY Aw, s'at what it is?

INA Wull ye stoap leerin' at them? Whit they gonnae think? Wur desperate ur somethin'?

MINNIE We've been staunin' here fur the last fifteen dances . . . wur desperate.

INA Aye, but ye don't want tae let oan . . .

JACKIE Wull you stoap gaun oan aboot Ina and Minnie an' come ower an' ask these dolls fur a dance?

TOMMY Awright, but Ah still think . . .

JACKIE C'mon . . .

*They saunter across the hall.*

INA Thur comin' ower! Here, this is better than sittin' at home watchin' *Come Dancin'* . . . intit?

MINNIE Jackie an' Tommy'll kill us if they fun oot . . . but aye! It is!!!

*The gents approach and stop . . . all four pull out their specs and put them on.*

TOMMY Ina!

INA Tommy!

JACKIE Minnie!

MINNIE Jackie!

# FATHER'S BLESSING

## *by Laurie Rowley*

FATHER Rikki Fulton; MOTHER Juliet Cadzow;
DAUGHTER Judy Sweeney; ROBERT Tony Roper

*A living room. The father is pacing the room and occasionally glancing at his watch.*

FATHER Look at the time! Where the hell is she?

MOTHER (*knitting on the sofa*) It is New Year's Eve, Dad.

FATHER I don't care! No daughter of mine stays out till this time. I'll murder her when she comes in.

*The door opens and the daughter enters.*

DAUGHTER Hello Mum, Dad, I'm home.

FATHER Where the hell have you been till this time?

DAUGHTER There's someone I'd like you to meet.

*She brings in a scruffy, bearded student type, wearing jeans.*

FATHER What the hell is that?

DAUGHTER This is Robert.

FATHER Robert? You mean . . . it's human?

DAUGHTER Dad! Robert's asked me to marry him.

FATHER What???

DAUGHTER . . . and we want your blessing.

FATHER Ha, ha! You want to marry an extra-terrestrial rubbish tip and you're asking for my blessing?

DAUGHTER Yes, Dad.

FATHER Don't be stupid, girl, you think I'd approve of you marrying an . . . an adolescent wino? (*To lad*) Spend your dole money on cider, do you, son?

DAUGHTER He's not on the dole, Dad. He's an art student.

FATHER An art student! That's even worse than being on the dole! Tell me this, fungus-face, how the hell is a destitute art student going to support my daughter, eh? Tell me that.

ROBERT (*very polite and well spoken*) Well, sir, apart from being an art student I'm also a major stockholder in my father's brewery.

FATHER (*short pause, then mood changes to beaming smiles as he shakes hands with the lad*) Welcome to the family, Robert my boy. Nice to meet you, here have a drink . . .

# THE JOYS OF MARRIED LIFE

●

## DISCOVERING EACH OTHER

### by Terry Ravenscroft

JOE Rikki Fulton; SUE Claire Nielson

*A hotel bedroom with a screen a few feet from a double bed. A pitcher of water and glasses stand on a cocktail cabinet near the bed.*

*Joe and Sue, a honeymoon couple, come into the room, Joe carrying Sue 'over the threshold'. In one hand he has a suitcase with 'Just Married' written on it. Sue is pretty, busty and blonde. Joe closes the door and puts Sue down. He grabs hold of her and kisses her passionately.*

JOE Get 'em off!

SUE (*smiles*) You're glad that I made you wait now, aren't you?

JOE Yes. Get 'em off!

SUE All in good time. After all, you've been patient with me for three years. Can't you wait a little longer?

JOE Yes, of course I can. (*He 'waits' for a second, then grabs her hand and makes for the bed*) That's long enough – come on!

SUE Give me a chance to undress first. Don't you want me to put on my sexy negligée, darling?

JOE  Yes – then I can take it off.

SUE  (*pushing him playfully*) You! (*Pecking him on the cheek*) Now, don't go away.

JOE  You must be joking.

*Sue goes behind the screen.*

JOE  (*putting the suitcase on the bed*) No! I'll no'!

*He takes out a pair of pyjamas and puts them back, then starts to take his tie off. In the meantime Sue has taken off her dress and hung it over the screen.*

JOE  (*he has a thought*) Er . . . Sue?

SUE  Yes?

JOE  Why HAVE you made me wait until after we were married?

SUE  Well, it's simply that most couples nowadays know everything there is to know about each other by the time they get married . . . (*her hand appears over the screen dangling a bra – she drops it on Joe's side of the screen*) . . . whereas we have the joy of discovering the mysteries of each other's bodies still to come.

*Joe enjoys the sexy performance with the bra and bends to pick it up.*

JOE  Yes I see what you mea . . .

*As he picks up the bra, two rubber falsies fall out. He picks them up and squeezes them.*

SUE  Oh, by the way – I think there's something you ought to know.

JOE  I think I've already found out (*'bouncing' one of the falsies in his hand*).

SUE  Really? (*She hangs a blonde wig over the corner of the screen*) You mean you already know that I wear a wig?

JOE  (*mouths to himself, shocked*) Wig?

*He turns to see the wig and goes over to the cocktail cabinet to pour himself a whisky and water.*

SUE  Is everything all right?

JOE  Yes . . . yes – I was just getting a glass of water.

SUE  Pardon?

JOE  I said I was just getting . . .

SUE You'll have to speak up – my hearing-aid seems to be on the blink again.

JOE (*mouths to himself*) Hearing-aid?

SUE What was it you were saying?

JOE (*louder*) I was just getting a glass of water.

SUE Pardon?

JOE (*he goes to the screen and holds up the glass of water*) Water

SUE Oh, thank you. How thoughtful of you.

*Sue's hand comes over the top of the screen and drops a pair of false teeth into the glass.*

JOE Er . . . Sue?

SUE Yes?

JOE I've been thinking.

SUE Yes?

JOE Well, it is still quite early. Why don't we go out for a stroll before we turn in?

SUE I'd rather not if you don't mind. We could go to the local hop if you like.

*She hangs an artificial leg over the other corner of the screen.*

SUE Ready. Close your eyes for a big surprise.

JOE (*to himself*) You can say that again.

SUE Are they closed?

JOE Yes.

*He closes his eyes and begins to pray.*

SUE Here I come then.

*Sue appears from behind the screen. She is quite normal and dressed in a sexy negligée.*

SUE You can open them now.

*Joe opens one eye very cautiously. He sees Sue and looks amazed. He points at her and jabbers.*

SUE (*bursting out laughing*) Your face!

JOE But . . . but what about . . .? (*He points at the teeth in the glass*) and . . .? (*Pointing at the wig*) and . . .? (*Pointing at the artificial leg*)

SUE All a joke. Your best man put me up to it.

JOE I'll kill him! I'll murder him! Just wait till I get my hands . . . (*he calms down*) Not that it would have made any difference of course. I mean I would still love you even if you did happen to be dropping to bits.

SUE (*cuddles him*) And I'd still love you even if you were dropping to bits.

JOE  You really mean that, don't you?

SUE  Of course I do darling.

JOE  Good. It's just as well. Can you hold that?

*He takes off his toupee to reveal that he is bald. Then he hands the wig to Sue, who looks horrified.*

JOE  Will you undo these? They've been killing me. (*He begins to remove his corset*) Be gentle with me darling.

*Sue looks even more appalled.*

JOE  Oh, and here – keep your eye on this.

*He removes his glass eye – and Sue faints.*

# ASPIRIN

## *by Quentin Reynolds*

### HUSBAND Rikki Fulton; WIFE Juliet Cadzow

*A bedroom. A woman is lying on her back sleeping in bed. Her mouth is wide open and she is snoring loudly. Her husband, dressed in his pyjamas, is seen to pour a glass of water. Then he takes two aspirins from a bottle. He walks over, glass in hand, and drops the two aspirins into the woman's gaping mouth. She wakes up spluttering.*

WIFE  Wh . . .? Whit's happening? (*He hands her the glass of water*)

HUSBAND  Drink that, hen.

*She drinks the water.*

WIFE  Whit wiz that I swallowed?

HUSBAND  It wiz two aspirins, hen.

WIFE  (*puzzled*) But Ah've not goat a headache.

HUSBAND  (*rubbing his hands together with relish*) Ho, ho!! Ya Beauty!

*He leaps on to the bed.*

60

# THE VISIT

## *by Bob Black*

GUARD Tony Roper; PRISONER Gregor Fisher; WIFE Rikki Fulton

*The visiting area in a prison, with a Christmas wreath saying 'Arrest ye merry gentlemen' on the wall. A door opens and a guard brings in the rather sullen prisoner, wrestling him over to a chair and bundling him down on to it.*

PRISONER I don't want a visitor.

GUARD Shut up. Now you just sit there and behave! Your visitor will be here in a minute.

*The guard exits. A door opens on the other side of the wire, and the prisoner's dumpy, plain, over-emotional wife enters. The prisoner doesn't seem overjoyed to see her.*

PRISONER Oh, it's you.

*The wife stands at the door. She is very emotional, trying hard not to cry and hardly able to speak. She hovers on the brink of breaking down and dissolving completely into tears.*

WIFE H-Hullo, Wullie. I'm . . . I'm (*very emotionally*) Oh I'm that happy to see you!! (*She comes over to the wire, but doesn't sit*) What are we going to do?

PRISONER I don't know about you, hen, but I'm gonnae do eighteen months.

WIFE (*sitting*) That's just like you, Wullie! (*Blows her nose loudly*) You always were dead selfish!!

PRISONER What do'you mean? Selfish!?

WIFE What about me? Me!? Stuck in that single-end wi' eight weans, my parents, your sister, her fancy-man AND his Pomeranian. We're crowded out! I don't know how we'd have made ends meet if I hadn't taken in a lodger.

PRISONER A lodger!? Here. I hope he's no' in MY bed!

WIFE No. He's in the bath.

PRISONER The bath? What have ye done with the coal?

WIFE  That's in your bed.

PRISONER  (*displeased*) Oh, that's nice, that is! Ye mean my bed's full of great lumps of dirty, manky, nutty slack all day!?

WIFE  (*sighing, fondly and emotionally*) Aye. It's just like having you at home.

PRISONER  (*sullen*) Huh! That's just about all you think o' me, isn't it!

WIFE  That's not fair, Wullie. I've made you a good wife.

PRISONER  You've never even made me a good dinner!!

WIFE  Night after night I've put hot food on that table!

PRISONER  And night after night I telt ye to put it on a plate first!!

WIFE  (*threatening to bubble over*) Don't you . . . don't you start on me! I've been a good mother to all your children! Aye and to the two that aren't yours!

PRISONER  (*shocked*) What!?

WIFE  (*playing the martyr*) The nights they've lain in their beds greeting and screaming, and me almost too tired to drag myself upstairs to belt them to sleep. Then you'd wake up in front of the telly complainin' about the noise and you nailing your cod and chips to the wall. I tell you, Wullie, when I laid you out cold wi' that dining room chair it was for your own good! (*Growing more emotional*) And what thanks do I get? Eh? Some Christmas this is gonnae be! What am I supposed to say to the weans? 'Hush pet. Hush. Santa cannae come this year, he was caught driving a getaway sledge.' That's very nice, eh. I was . . . I was just so upset when they came to tell me ye were in jail.

PRISONER (*surprised and touched*) No?

WIFE Aye. They called right in the middle of *Dallas*, so they did.

PRISONER (*annoyed, getting to his feet*) Aye. That's right! Blame me! I was only doin' some last-minute Christmas shopping! But I'd no sooner chipped the brick through Littlewoods' window when the polis jumped me! They were waitin' for me, see? I had a price on my head!

WIFE (*sighing sadly*) If only ye'd had a brain in it, too. Whatever made ye do it?

PRISONER (*goes and pounds on door*) I'll tell ye! I WANTED to get caught! That's what made me do it! I wanted to get put in here, well away from you – ya stupid, senile old cow!

WIFE (*dreadfully hurt, close to tears, choking with emotion*) Oh Wullie, Wullie, that's a terrible thing to say!

*The guard opens the door and enters. The wife stands.*

PRISONER And now I wish I'd never done it! Cos see this place? It stinks! We're over-crowded! Under-heated! The food's rotten, the bed's hard, I'm never allowed out and I get knocked about senseless every morning, noon and night.

WIFE (*brightening up*) Oh Wullie. That makes me feel a whole lot better.

PRISONER (*baffled*) Eh?

WIFE At least you've got all your home comforts.

*This is the last straw. The prisoner rushes towards his wife but the guard grabs him and takes him out of the room. The wife waves goodbye.*

# THE WAITING GAME
## *by Bob Black*

DRUNK Rikki Fulton; MAN (expectant father) Tony Roper; NURSE Annette Staines

*A sign on a wall says: 'Maternity Waiting Room'. It's a typical waiting room with chairs against the walls, a main door and a pair of double doors as well. A very nervous man (the expectant father) is constantly pacing to and fro across the room. He looks drawn and very anxious. In through the main doors comes a second man, very drunk! He is swaying and staggering, can hardly stay upright or focus on anything.*

DRUNK Hullo! Hullo! Here we are again!

*The nervous man keeps pacing to and fro . . . the drunk watches him pacing . . . the motion begins to make him feel sick. Eventually he can't take it any more!*

DRUNK Here, pal, gonnae stop that? You're makin' me feel kind've sick . . .

MAN Oh. I'm sorry. I'm very sorry. I'm just a bit nervous. It's my first time, you see.

DRUNK (*very surprised*) First time? Is it? Your first time? Ach, don't worry, son. I've been in here dozens of times. I'll see you all right . . .

MAN (*worried*) The waiting's the worst bit, isn't it?

DRUNK No, it's actually the waiting that's the worst. But don't you worry, pal. I've never had anything go wrong in here . . .

MAN Good.

DRUNK Except once.

*From now on, everything the drunk says only serves to worry the man more and more.*

DRUNK My first time! I wis in here, waiting, right? And just as they carried mine oot tae me . . . they drapped it!

MAN (*shocked*) What!?

DRUNK They drapped it! (*Points down*) Right there! Oan the floor! What an uproar! Of course, they wis full o' apologies, but that's no' the point, is it? (*The man is appalled*) Anyway, there wis no harm done, they just took it away and brought us another one.

MAN (*shaken*) That . . . that's terrible! (*Fearing the worst*)

DRUNK But I'll . . . I'll tell ye what's even worse, son! When they gi'e ye the wrong wan! Aye! See, the time before last, they gie'd us someone else's. SOMEONE ELSE'S! I mean, we didnae know. We never realised till we got it home and opened it up.

MAN (*even more appalled*) Oh God, that's awful!

DRUNK I mean, I'd have come right back and complained there and then! But well, it wis a long way an' it had started rainin'. So in the end we just kept it.

MAN (*even more shocked*) What!? You kept it!!

DRUNK An' I tell you, the way it turned oot, we were glad we did. And anyway, naebody here bothered their bum!

MAN (*very anxious, desperate for reassurance*) But surely that doesn't happen very often?

DRUNK Hardly ever! Don't worry, son. Hardly ever. But I'll gie ye a wee tip. See, when they bring yours oot . . . if it's no quite what ye set yer heart on, don't say a word! Cos . . . cos they'll go for ye!

MAN (*alarmed*) What!?

DRUNK There wis a fight in here once, cos o' that VERY thing! There wis a guy didnae get whit he an' his wife wanted, and they hit him with it!

MAN Oh, no!!

DRUNK Beat him senseless wi' it.

MAN (*hiding his face in his hands*) No! No! Don't tell me any more!

DRUNK They flung it at him . . . It bounced aff that wall and landed right . . . (*he looks round for the exact spot*) . . . landed right . . . (*looks round again, puzzled – the man beside him is weeping, sobbing into his hands; the Drunk takes a hard, puzzled, drunken look at the room*) Here, wait a minute! I'm in the wrong place! This is nae the Tandoori Take-Away at all! This must be the Shish Mahal.

*Just then a nurse comes through the double doors, carrying a baby in a blanket.*

NURSE Mr Brown? Congratulations. It's a boy . . .

*Desperately relieved and thankful, the nervous man hurries over and takes the baby. He holds it lovingly, cradling it in his arms, relieved and grateful.*

MAN Oh, thank you! Thank you! Thank you!

*The drunk staggers by and looks into the blanket.*

DRUNK Oh, here. Ye must be kiddin', son. You'll never eat all that!

*He staggers away very drunkenly.*

# PUTTING THE BOOT IN

.

## AFTER THE PARTY

*by Laurie Rowley*

CHARLIE Rikki Fulton; SAMMY Gregor Fisher

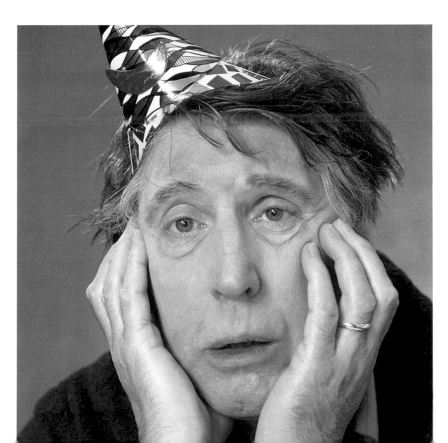

*A kitchen on New Year's morning. It's obvious that a party took place the night before. There are empty bottles, half-finished plates of food, etc.*

*A man is at the sink. The inner door slowly opens and Charlie is there, wearing a dressing-gown and looking absolutely dog-rough with a hangover. He leans on the door frame.*

SAMMY  Morning.

CHARLIE  (*long moan*) Eeaarghh!

SAMMY  Oh! Morning, Charlie. How are you?

CHARLIE  Eaargh! What time is it?

SAMMY  Just after eleven.

CHARLIE  What day is it?

SAMMY  New Year's Day!

CHARLIE  What year is it?

SAMMY  Dear, oh dear, you did have a good time last night, didn't you? Come on, sit down and I'll make you a cup of coffee.

CHARLIE  (*slowly sitting at the table*) Wait a minute . . . who are you?

SAMMY  (*laughing*) I'm your brother. Sammy.

CHARLIE  Sammy who?

*Sammy shakes his head in mild exasperation and returns to the coffee-making.*

CHARLIE  Here. Did they manage to catch the farmer?

SAMMY  Farmer?

CHARLIE  The one who ran over me with his combine harvester!

SAMMY  Eh? You weren't run over, Charlie.

CHARLIE  You tell that to my body!

SAMMY  We had a party last night. Don't you remember?

CHARLIE  A party? All I can remember is a terrible dream I had.

SAMMY  A dream?

CHARLIE  Aye. I dreamed I was shovin' my wife's mother head-first down the toilet.

SAMMY  Oh, that wasn't a dream.

CHARLIE  What?

68

SAMMY You did shove her down the toilet. You were pretending to be the captain of the *Titanic*, shouting 'Women and children first!'

CHARLIE My God! My wife'll kill me when she gets up!

SAMMY Don't worry about it – your wife's not here.

CHARLIE Not here?

SAMMY No. She went off with those police frogmen to Greenock.

CHARLIE Police frogmen? Greenock?

SAMMY Aye. They're waiting for your mother-in-law to come out the other end of the pipes.

CHARLIE Oh, no! Where's my keys!? I'd better get out there in the car!

SAMMY Eh . . . what car?

CHARLIE My BMW in the drive.

SAMMY Oh, that BMW. Do you not remember the one you lost in the card game?

CHARLIE What card game?

SAMMY You remember! Billy Smith had a full house.

CHARLIE And what did I have?

SAMMY Mrs Paterson, the Baker's Wife.

*Charlie groans again and puts his head in his hands. Then he realises something and looks round the kitchen.*

CHARLIE Wait a minute – here. This isnae my house!

SAMMY Of course it isn't. No, no, it's mine. Yours was burnt to the ground when you set off the fireworks, remember? Just after you told me that you didn't have any insurance, and just before the fire brigade ran over your dog!

CHARLIE (*putting his head in his hands*) Oh, no! I don't believe all this . . .

SAMMY Ach, come on! It's not as bad as all that! Look on the bright side!

CHARLIE The bright side?!

SAMMY Aye! Look what you won in the raffle we had at the party!

*From beside the sink he takes a large bottle of whisky and hands it to Charlie. Charlie looks sick.*

# OF COURSE I REMEMBER YOU

## by Rikki Fulton

GIRL Annette Staines; SIR GREGOR Gregor Fisher;
MAN Rikki Fulton

*Outside the Theatre Royal. Sir Gregor is signing an autograph for a young girl. He finishes with a flourish and hands back the book with a benign smile.*

GIRL  Oh, thank you so much, Sir Gregor. I'm SUCH an admirer of yours. In my opinion you're Europe's greatest actor.

SIR GREGOR  (*bowing*) My dear child. Obviously a young lady of discernment and good taste.

GIRL  I hope you didn't mind me asking you.

SIR GREGOR  Not at all, dear lady. Not at all. I NEVER mind. Depending, of course, on how I am approached.

MAN  Well, hullaw-rerr!

*The girl hurries away. Man comes up and sticks his face up into Sir Gregor's.*

MAN  You'll no' remember me!

SIR GREGOR  Remember you? I can't even focus on you!

MAN  Oh, sorry. But here, d'ye no' remember? No' mind aboot eight years ago ye were doon in London, and ye went tae a party in St John's Wood, and a fella gave ye a lift home in his Jaguar?

SIR GREGOR  (*laughing*) Ha, ha, ha! Good heavens. Was that YOU?

MAN  Ha, ha, ha! Naw! But mind ye asked this fella intae yer hotel for a drink, an' the HEAD PORTER came up an' tellt ye ye couldnae huv wan.

SIR GREGOR  Of course, now I remember. You were the head porter.

MAN  Naw! But mind ye had a terrific argument, and eventually they hud tae send for a POLISMAN.

SIR GREGOR  The ... er ... polisman?

MAN  Naw! But you were that angry ye stomped up tae yer room an' ye banged yer door that hard it jammed shut, an' ye hud tae send fur a CHAMBERMAID.

*Sir Gregor looks and wonders.*

MAN  Naw! But ... remember ... they hud tae 'phone aboot a dozen JOINERS afore ye could get wan to come an' let ye oot.

SIR GREGOR  (*remembering, laughing and pointing at the man*) Ahhhhhh!

MAN  (*laughing happily*) AYE! Ah wis wan o' the joiners that couldnae come!

# THE CURRIES
## *by Bob Black*

RONNIE Gregor Fisher; ROY Rikki Fulton; MC Tony Roper

*The Lavvymore Hotel. On stage in the hotel's cabaret room an MC is introducing the next act.*

MC Ladies and gentlemen. With great pride, and at very little cost, the Hotel Lavvymore presents that sensational Scottish singing duo . . . The Curries.

*On stage, to applause, come The Curries. They are typical Scottish folk-singer types, wearing leather waistcoats and shirt sleeves rolled up. Roy carries a mandolin, Ronnie carries a guitar.*
*Ronnie goes to the front of the stage, to address the audience. Roy stands in the background and nods his approval.*

RONNIE (*in a broad Scots accent, perfectly serious*) We'd like to begin with a song we've composed about the Glencoe Massacre. It was a brutal time, when brother butchered brother . . . when men hacked bits off other men . . . when soldiers with dirty great long swords disembowelled other soldiers whose swords weren't quite as long!

*In the background, Roy is beginning to feel a bit squeamish.*

RONNIE It was a time when rivers ran with blood, and oozing entrails stained the heather!

*Roy is now definitely feeling ill, swallowing hard, and trying not to be sick. Ronnie presses on regardless.*

RONNIE The chorus we've written goes . . .

*He doesn't sing but speaks it with relish and bloodthirsty enthusiasm.*

'They grabbed his head and severed it,
and then ripped out his tongue!
It wriggled like a jellied eel
on the ground where it was flung!
They beat his brain to a throbbing mush
and slashed his guts asunder!
Then cut his heart out with a dirk!
And he died . . . no bloody wonder!'

*In the background, Roy is in big trouble. He is nauseous, sagging and unsteady on his feet.*

RONNIE That's the chorus. So please, do sing along! The song is called 'The Splattered Blood of Our Slaughtered Sons!' (*Ready to start, counting the song in brightly*) Right Roy. An ah-one, an ah-two, and ...

*Behind him Roy gulps, reels slightly and collapses to the floor in a dead faint!*

# SEMI-TOUGH

## *by Mick Deasy*

FIRST HARD MAN Steven Pinder;
SECOND HARD MAN Rikki Fulton; MAD MICK Gregor Fisher

*A public bar. Two hard men stand at the bar, with bottles in front of them. A third man enters and orders a bottle of beer.*

FIRST HARD MAN Gawd, look who's just walked in.

SECOND HARD MAN Who?

FIRST HARD MAN Mad Mick MacDonald. He's the dirtiest, meanest hard man in Glasgow. Drink up, let's get out of here.

SECOND HARD MAN Wait a minute ... stay where you are ... we'll see who is the dirtiest, meanest hard man in Glasgow.

*He approaches Mad Mick and slaps him on the shoulder. Mad Mick turns around and the hard man breaks a bottle on the table.*

SECOND HARD MAN Are you Mad Mick MacDonald?

*Without looking at him, Mad Mick picks up his bottle, bites off the neck, spits out the glass and runs his thumb round the jagged edge. The second hard man watches in amazement.*

MAD MICK Aye.

SECOND HARD MAN Can you tell me the right time, please?

# THREE WISHES

## *by Quentin Reynolds*

TAM Tony Roper; BERT Rikki Fulton

*A public bar. Bert is standing at the bar. He is dressed in Bermuda shorts and sunglasses. All around him stand the locals, dressed for a winter's evening in coats, scarves and hats. Bert is approached by Tam who is dressed like the locals.*

TAM (*giving Bert's shorts and sunglasses the once over*) Whit happened to you?

BERT Well, you know how Ah saved Mr McAllister's wee dug frae drowning?

TAM McAllister the millionaire?

BERT Aye. Well, in gratitude he gave me three wishes.

TAM Whit did ye ask fur?

BERT First, Ah said, Ah want tae get away frae Scotland tae where the sun is shining.

TAM Whit did he dae?

BERT Put me oan the first plane tae Bermuda . . . there Ah wis, standing wi ma raincoat an' bunnet, oan a sandy beach. So Ah asked him tae dress me in aw the clobber.

TAM (*indicating Bert's Bermuda shorts, etc.*) Well Ah can see that that wish wis granted . . . but whit was your last wish?

BERT Ah asked him tae arrange it so's Ah'd never work again.

TAM Right, right. So whit did he do?

BERT He put me oan the next plane back tae Scotland.

# FROSTBITE

## by Mick Deasy

DOCTOR Rikki Fulton; BLOKE Gregor Fisher

*A hospital clinic. A doctor, wearing a white coat, is sitting at his desk. There is a knock at the door.*

DOCTOR Come in . . .

*A sorry-looking bloke walks in.*

DOCTOR . . . Yes?

BLOKE The sister told me to come and see you about my wife, Doctor.

DOCTOR Mr . . .?

BLOKE Carter.

DOCTOR Carter? Carter? Ah yes, your wife was the chronic constipation case complicated by severe frostbite.

BLOKE My wife is the one who fell asleep in the outside toilet.

DOCTOR (*opens file*) I think you'd better sit down, Mr Carter. I'm afraid I have some bad news.

BLOKE She's not dead, is she, Doctor?

DOCTOR No, no, no . . . not dead exactly . . . but, er, when we got her down to the theatre we found that the frostbite was far worse than anticipated and we had to carry out quite extensive surgery . . .

BLOKE You mean . . . you had to amputate?

DOCTOR Actually, most of it just snapped off. But yes, clinically speaking, it could be described as amputation.

BLOKE Oh, no, what was it, Doctor? One of her fingers?

DOCTOR Partly.

BLOKE Was it more than one finger?

DOCTOR Yes.

BLOKE Not a whole arm?

DOCTOR No.

BLOKE Oh, thank God!

DOCTOR It was two whole arms . . . and you know the legs were affected and er . . .

BLOKE And? You mean there's more?

DOCTOR Well, rather less actually.

BLOKE Look, Doctor, I want to see my wife now.

DOCTOR Very well, but I must warn you that she won't be as you remember her.

*He takes a shoebox out of his bottom drawer and places it on his desk. He opens it to reveal a nose on a bed of cotton wool. The two men stare at the nose. The bloke picks up the box, looks underneath, under the desk, in the drawer, etc.*

BLOKE Where's the rest of her?

DOCTOR I did say that the surgery was quite extensive.

BLOKE But that's just her nose . . . (*he stares down at the nose*) Daphne? Daphne? Daphne? (*Shouting*)

DOCTOR She can't hear you, Mr Carter.

BLOKE Is that the effects of the anaesthetic, Doctor?

DOCTOR No, it's because she hasn't any ears, Mr Carter.

BLOKE Do you think she . . .?

*The bloke puts his head in his hands and starts sobbing.*

DOCTOR Oh yes she knows. There's something I haven't told you concerning your wife.

BLOKE (*still sobbing*) What?

DOCTOR (*looking at the table*) I don't quite know how to put this . . . the operations weren't a complete success.

BLOKE (*also looking at the nose*) How do you mean?

DOCTOR Your wife has lost her sense of smell.

BLOKE She'll be just like a vegetable.

DOCTOR Part of a vegetable . . . but there's no reason why with proper care and attention, it, I mean she, shouldn't carry on breathing as long as you or I.

BLOKE Yes, well, I love my wife, Doctor, and I intend to take her home and make her as comfortable as possible.

DOCTOR That's the spirit. Boracic, lint, plenty of cotton wool and a spot of make-up will make her feel a different woman.

BLOKE Yes, you're right, Doctor.

DOCTOR Good. Excellent. (*He puts the lid back on the box*) There you are. (*Handing the box to the bloke*) Oh, do you want to take her as she is or shall I wrap her for you?

# RECOGNITION

## *by Laurie Rowley*

DIGNITARY Rikki Fulton; MAN Tony Roper;
HOTEL GUESTS Extras

*A hotel lounge. A dignitary stands with a well-to-do group. He is airing his views very self-importantly and is obviously a pillar of local society.*

DIGNITARY . . . so I said to Prince Charles, 'Here you are, sir, use mine, it's cocked and ready for firing . . .'

*The guests laugh in approval and the dignitary singles out a man in the group.*

DIGNITARY  Excuse me, sir, haven't we met before?

MAN  No, I don't think so.

DIGNITARY  Oh, come now, come now, I never forget a face. Now, where was it . . .

MAN  I really don't remember.

DIGNITARY  Oh but I know you, I know you so well. Tell me, what do you do?

MAN  I manage the sex shop in Morningside.

DIGNITARY  *(quickly)* Never seen you before in my life!

# NOT SATISFIED

## *by Kenneth Rock*

FIRST MAN Tony Roper; SECOND MAN Gregor Fisher

*A pub, with various people in the bar.*

FIRST MAN  What's the matter with you? You look more miserable than ever this evening.

SECOND MAN  I've got this personal problem.

FIRST MAN  What is it?

SECOND MAN  I can't tell you – it's personal. Besides, it's embarrassing.

FIRST MAN  Come on, you can tell me. That's what mates are for.

SECOND MAN  You're right. You see, the problem is – I can't satisfy my wife.

FIRST MAN  I see. (*Thinks*) Have you ever tried blowing in her left ear, caressing her shoulder with your fingertips and tickling her tummy with a feather duster?

SECOND MAN  (*shocked*) No – she wouldnae like that!

FIRST MAN  Aye, she does.

  *The second man looks puzzled – then he realises . . .*

# CREATURES GREAT AND SMALL

•

## BILLY

*by Mike Radford*

FIRST MAN Gregor Fisher; SECOND MAN Tony Roper

*Sinister music. A man dressed as a gangster sits in a darkened room. Another gangster comes in.*

FIRST MAN  The cops have got Billy.

SECOND MAN  What? He only got out yesterday.

FIRST MAN  He went straight round there this morning.

SECOND MAN  I guess being caged up must have gone to his head. Will he talk?

FIRST MAN  Of course he won't. Billy's no talker, you know that.

SECOND MAN  Even so, I think we ought to play safe . . .

FIRST MAN  Come on . . . Billy's no stool pigeon. If the cops want anything . . . he'll let them whistle for it . . . Relax, Billy's never talked in his life . . .

*There is a ring at the door. The first man answers it and returns.*

SECOND MAN  Who was it?

FIRST MAN  The cops. They dropped Billy off.

SECOND MAN  Did he talk?

FIRST MAN  Of course he didn't.

*He brings out a budgie.*

Did you Billy?

# THE BUDGIE

## *by John Byrne*

BUDGIE Rikki Fulton; HOUSEWIFE Margo Cunningham;
VISITOR Claire Nielson

*A living room. A housewife puts seed into a bird cage and closes the
door. The budgie (Rikki in costume) is in the cage.*

BUDGIE  Thank God she's away an' gei'in us peace. Ma claws is
killin' us, so they ur. Up and doon that stupit ladder aw day . . . gei'in
that wee bell a dunt wi' ma heid. 'Who's a pretty boy, then? Who's a
pretty . . .' Ah'll gie her 'Who's a pretty boy then'! Whit dis she think
Ah'm ur? Eh? A ravin' . . .? Oh, oh . . . here she comes. Better tuck

the aul' nut under the wing. If she sees Ah'm still awake she'll huv us jumpin' through that stupit-lookin' plastic ring . . . an' dookin' ma heid intae the watter an' splashing it aw err ma ferras . . . 's bloody freezin' . . . she's got visitors. (*He tucks his head under his wing*)

HOUSEWIFE Come on, Monty. Do our wee trick for Mrs McCusker. Oh, he's sleeping, the wee soul.

*The housewife and her visitor go away.*

BUDGIE Is that her away? Oh, thank God. See when there's people in . . . visitors . . . ma life's no worth livin' naer it is. Come on, Monty, do our wee trick for Mrs McCusker. Our wee trick! I'd like to see her on this bloody swing. Mind you, it's some trick that. She had me do it for the minister the other day . . . a triple somersault right affy the top perch there. Right up there . . . intae the watter trough . . . that's some height that . . . right intae the watter. Soaked to the skin, Ah was . . . Him an' her jist laughed. Ah gave them a mouthful but . . . Whit? She was black affrontit . . . said Ah'd picked it up frae the big Macaw upstairs . . . S'no' true – it's her . . . She swerrs like a trooper, she dis! Ye want tae hear her when her man comes hame wi' a good bucket in him . . . Whit? Big Macaw upstairs wid turn scarlet if he could hear the language . . . an' he's been tae sea. Hey, know whit he gets fur his tea, the big Macaw? Choclit biscuits! Choclit biscuits! Last time Ah seen a choclit biscuit wis oor Chrissie's weddin' . . . an' Ah never goat a smell ae wan . . . never a smell. Aul' greedy-guts scoffed the lot. 'Did ye give oor Monty a wee bit a biscuit, Faither?' 'Course a did,' says he. 'Gie'd him hauf the packet. Near had the haun affy us.' Bloody liar! Aye Ah could fair go a choclit biscuit the noo, steid ae that Budgie-Brek. Budgie-Brek . . . honest tae God. She seen it on the TV. 'Aw here, oor Monty wid like that, widn't he, Faither? Luk at that wee budgie oan the TV. He's the picture of health.' Picture of health, ma tail ferras! He wis stuffed! Stuffed! An' she couldnae even tell . . . he wis aw padded oot . . . wee roon belly . . . gless eyes shinin' away . . . tied oan tae a perch an' bein' shove back an' furrit by some guy oot a camera range. Thur awffy glaikit people, urn't they? So that's aw Ah've hud tae eat ever since . . . 1964, that wis . . . 1964. Aye, it's changed days. Ah mind the time she used tae let us oot fur a fly roon the scullery . . . wance a week . . . Aw, thon wis magic . . . up roon the pulley . . . zoom ower the sink . . . an' divebomb the aul' man at his dinner . . . used tae choke oan his tea. 'If Ah get ma hauns oan that wee blue basket Ah'll wring its bloody neck, so Ah will!' Whit a terr! Ah don't envy them doos an' seagulls an' sparras an' that, oot there . . . Ah'm really quite cosy here . . . three meals a day . . . even if it's that Budgie-Brek . . . s'nice an' warm . . . drap a sherry in the watter at Christmas . . . Aw, Ah mean, Ah cannae really complain. Here, is that hur comin' back? Hus she goat ma cover? Wish Ah hudnae kiddit oan Ah wis sleepin'. Oh, hell, Ah wis wantin' tae watch *Neighbours*.

*The housewife puts the cover over the cage.*

# MOTHS

## *by Frank Rodgers*

FIRST MOTH Gregor Fisher; SECOND MOTH Rikki Fulton;
MAN Tony Roper

*A living room with a moth fluttering around a lightbulb. A man is reading but glancing at the moth in irritation. The second moth is lounging, hands behind head, at the base of a table lamp. He is sitting on a Spanish travel brochure and wearing sunglasses. He opens a lunchbox and eats. The first moth lands beside him.*

FIRST MOTH  Hullo there.

SECOND MOTH  (*removing his sunglasses*) Hullo.

FIRST MOTH  You a new moth around here then?

SECOND MOTH  Aye.

FIRST MOTH  What're you doing?

SECOND MOTH  Nothing, just having my elevenses. Fancy a wee bit of carpet?

FIRST MOTH  No thanks. How come you're not up there flying round the lightbulb like the rest of us?

SECOND MOTH  What's the point?

FIRST MOTH  What's the point? In flying round the lightbulb? What are you saying man? Moths are born to fly round lightbulbs, aren't they? It's what we do, intit? I mean, it's our purpose in life, is it not?

SECOND MOTH  It's not my purpose. I think it's stupid.

FIRST MOTH  Stupid?

84

SECOND MOTH  Listen, pal, I've done my share of lightbulb fluttering and not just round 60 watt Mazdas either, son . . . I once fluttered round the floodlights at Hampden Park, so I did, until one night I got hit with the ball.

FIRST MOTH  What was the ball doing up there?

SECOND MOTH  They let Big John Greig take a penalty. So I don't flutter round lightbulbs any more; it's daft.

FIRST MOTH  So you just sit here all the time then?

SECOND MOTH  Not all the time no – on Thursday I go out to cash my Giro cheque.

FIRST MOTH  Och, you're a disgrace to hardworking moths, so you are . . . you're a revolutionary that's what. I bet you come from behind the iron curtain.

SECOND MOTH  Listen, there's nothing left-wing about me. Fancy a bit of semmit?

FIRST MOTH  No thanks.

SECOND MOTH  Marks and Spencers.

FIRST MOTH  No. Oh, listen, why don't you come and join us? It's great fun.

SECOND MOTH  Fun? You call getting your bum burnt on a hot lightbulb fun? I suppose you think it's hilarious when you batter your head off the lightshade? I suppose you die laughing when some idiot with a rolled-up magazine chases you round the room with the sole intention of flattening you against the wallpaper?

FIRST MOTH  Well no . . .

SECOND MOTH  I tell you there's more to life than hiding in wardrobes eating nothing but fur coats all day.

FIRST MOTH  Knickers!

SECOND MOTH  Aye, them and all, when I'm really hungry. You see, I want to travel, meet foreign moths, fly to Spain, do the Slosh in a Spanish disco, lie in the sun, drive fast cars . . .

FIRST MOTH  Drive fast cars – what, you?

SECOND MOTH  Aye, have you never heard of Stirling Moth? Fancy a bit of sock?

FIRST MOTH  Are they fresh?

SECOND MOTH  Last night's.

FIRST MOTH  Oh no, gives me terrible heartburn. (*Becoming interested*) So how do you plan to get to Spain then?

SECOND MOTH  I'm going to stow away in a suitcase when they go on their holidays. Just think, a couple of days chewing your way through lightweight suits and designer beachwear, all that nouvelle cuisine and then . . . hello sunshine!

FIRST MOTH  Oh, you beauty, that sounds brilliant. Can I come too?

SECOND MOTH  Certainly. Fancy a bit of brassière.

FIRST MOTH  No, too filling.

SECOND MOTH  You stick with me pal and you'll get such an attractive suntan you'll have all the Red Admirals in Spain trying to get you into bed.

FIRST MOTH  Great . . .

BOTH  (*singing*) Oh tonight we're off to sunny Spain, Hey Viva Esp . . .

*Suddenly the man slams a rolled-up magazine on to the table. The moths are holding their battered heads.*

SECOND MOTH  Ooya! D'ye fancy an Askit powder?

# SCOTS ABROAD

•

# FOOTBALL FANS
## *by Bob Black*

FIRST SUPPORTER Tony Roper;
SECOND SUPPORTER Rikki Fulton; NURSE Annette Staines

*A hospital ward in London. In a bed near the door sits Tony, a Scottish football supporter. He wears pyjamas, a tartan scarf and a rosette. His head is bandaged across the forehead, over his ears and under his chin. On top of the heavy bandage he wears a tartan tammy or bunnet.*

*In the next bed is another fan. He wears a Scottish football jersey and is also bedecked in tartan scarves and a couple of huge rosettes. He has one leg in splints and his arm in a sling. He is very indignant and irate, protesting and shouting all the way. A nurse takes his pulse.*

SECOND SUPPORTER  Here we go! Here we go! . . . Here we go! . . . Foul! Send him aff!! Ye sassenach assassins, ye! (*He moans in pain*) Ohhh Mammy!

NURSE  He's just coming round now.

*The nurse exits.*

FIRST SUPPORTER  Hullo therr, how's it goin'?

SECOND SUPPORTER  How's it going? I'm in hoaspital, that's how it's goin'.

FIRST SUPPORTER  What happened to you?

SECOND SUPPORTER  Ach, me an the boys were having a drink or ten after the game, when this big Rastafarian frae Tottenham comes over and says oor team was rubbish and we must be stupit to support them. Stupit? Us? Stupit?

FIRST SUPPORTER  Naw!

SECOND SUPPORTER  So, I says, 'Right pal – ootside and say that.'

FIRST SUPPORTER  I bet that wiped the smile off his face.

SECOND SUPPORTER  Naw, naw, he wis all for it. So I stepped ootside and . . . (*grimaces in pain*) . . . that was my big mistake.

FIRST SUPPORTER  Did he beat you up?

SECOND SUPPORTER  No, the train was still moving!

*He lies back and begins moaning again.*

FIRST SUPPORTER  It's the same every year we play the English intit? I've landed in here so many times noo, I've got a season ticket. I ask fur this ward every year . . .

SECOND SUPPORTER  Whit fur!?

FIRST SUPPORTER  Wembley's just doon the road! Ye can hear the roar o' the crowd an' everything. 'Wis ye at the gemme yersel'?

SECOND SUPPORTER  Aye.

*The first supporter produces a half bottle from under his covers, takes a swig and hands it to the second supporter, who also takes a swig and returns it. The first supporter hides it again.*

FIRST SUPPORTER  How did we get on then?

SECOND SUPPORTER  Did ye no' see it like?

FIRST SUPPORTER  Naw. I wis laid oot before the start! I . . . I ran on tae the pitch and attacked the band. (*Shame-faced and emotional*) I don't know whit came over me. I jist lost the heid.

SECOND SUPPORTER  So I see . . .

FIRST SUPPORTER  Eh? (*Fingers his bandages*) Oh, aye. The bandleader caught me wan wi' his trumpet. (*Shrugs*) It coulda been worse.

SECOND SUPPORTER  Aye. Coulda been a tuba!

FIRST SUPPORTER  Anyway, how did we do? Did we win? Did John Greig play well?

SECOND SUPPORTER  John Greig! He hasnae played fur Scotland fur ten year!

FIRST SUPPORTER  (*surprised*) Has he no'? Well, I've no' actually seen a game since . . . (*pauses to consider*) . . . 1961! I aye tend tae get injured afore the kick-aff! Two year ago I got duffed up afore I even left Glasgow. An' the time afore that I goat a smack in the mooth while I 'wis still in my ain hoose.

SECOND SUPPORTER  (*matter of fact*) Oh. Ye're married then?

FIRST SUPPORTER  Aye. (*Brightens and looks eager*) Still, how wis the gemme? How did it go?

SECOND SUPPORTER  Aw, it was byootiful . . . the sky above the grun wis clear . . . not a single cloud . . . as the lads in daurk blue came lopin' gracefully oot the tunnel an' oantae the turf, knoakin' the ba frae wan tae the other . . . wee bit keepy-uppy here, wee bit feint an' weave there . . . then the Ref blew his whistle an' summoned the captains tae the centre circle . . . a toss of the coin . . . the decision wis made . . . we wur playin' wi' the wind in wur faces, but were we daunted? Wur we Dick . . . the whistle blaws . . . we're off! The crowd roars . . . the boys wur magic . . . poetry in motion . . . doon baith wings, feedin' the ba' intae the goal mooth . . . up an at them. We wur aw ower them.

FIRST SUPPORTER  And whit was the score.

SECOND SUPPORTER  We loast six nil!

# A LAUGH AN ETHNIC MINUTE

## by Andy Hamilton

SCOTSMAN Rikki Fulton; ABERDONIAN Bill Denniston;
IRISHMAN Gregor Fisher; JEWISH LANDLORD Tony Roper;
ENGLISHWOMAN Claire Nielson; WEST INDIAN Tony Osoba
(and Extras)

*A reasonably crowded pub. A Scotsman is leaning on the bar, trying to quieten everyone down.*

SCOTSMAN  No, sssh, no quiet listen, who wants to hear a good joke? You'll love this one, ssh, quiet, this is great, this, an absolute killer.

*He creases up as about ten assorted customers gather round him.*

SCOTSMAN  . . . it's a real scream. Ready? There's these two Aberdonians, y'know, so mean that they hang loo-paper out to dry. Anyway, these two Aberdonians . . .

ABERDONIAN  (*enormous*) I come from Aberdeen and I don't like Aberdonian jokes.

SCOTSMAN  Oh well, yes, but I mean, you . . . they're only meant in fun . . . a joke . . . just a joke. I'm sure you can take a joke, after all, it's a free country.

ABERDONIAN  True enough. You go ahead and tell your joke . . .

SCOTSMAN  Thanks . . .

ABERDONIAN  While I ring for an ambulance.

SCOTSMAN  Yes . . . um, well, there were these two Irishmen, you see.

ABERDONIAN  I thought you said Aberdonians.

SCOTSMAN  No, no, I've just remembered, that one's a different joke, not at all funny really, you know, one of those old jokes built around the popular myth that all Aberdonians are tall . . . and handsome. No, this one's definitely about two Irishmen, two incredibly stupid Irish . . .

*Two navvies move towards him threateningly.*

SCOTSMAN  Jews. In fact, Jews, who just happen to be living in Ireland.

IRISHMAN  And just what do you mean by that?

SCOTSMAN  On holiday. They're there on holiday. Anyway these two Jews, Moyshe and Hymie, are driving along in a car and . . .

*He empties his glass and calls to the other end of the bar.*

. . . another pint of 'heavy' please landlord . . . where was I?

*The Jewish landlord approaches.*

LANDLORD  (*very kosher*) You want 'heavy', we've got heavy.

SCOTSMAN  . . . and . . . er . . . anyway, these two West Indians. . .

IRISHMAN  West Indians?

SCOTSMAN  (*checks for black faces – there are none*) Yeah, you know, sambos.

IRISHMAN  Called Moyshe and Hymie?

SCOTSMAN  Imagine you remembering that! Well, you know what funny names those missionaries used to give them. Anyhow, one turns to the other and he says, 'Fit like', 'Begorrah' I mean 'hullor dere', 'cos like I said, you, they were two sambos and . . .

*The sound of an approaching steel band.*

. . . um . . . what's that?

LANDLORD  Oh that'll be the Black Power Reggae Ensemble. They come here to do a gig every lunchtime.

*The doors fly open and the reggae ensemble flood in. Greetings are exchanged.*

LANDLORD  Quiet lads, this fella's telling a joke.

SCOTSMAN  (*suddenly evasive*) Well no, please really, it wasn't particularly funny. Let's have some music shall we?

WEST INDIAN  Come on, man, let's hear the joke.

SCOTSMAN  Well . . . er . . . oh dear, I've lost the thread now. How about some music, eh?

IRISHMAN  You'd just got to the bit about the two nigger . . .

SCOTSMAN  -aguans! Of course, that's it, yes.

WEST INDIAN  Nicaraguans! Say, that's a coincidence. Sanchez here is Nicaraguan.

*The West Indian brings Sanchez forward. He is an enormous Nean-derthal hulk with a broken nose and cauliflower ears.*

SCOTSMAN  I see . . . well, these two Nicaraguans . . . um . . . hitch a lift with these two . . . er . . . two Swedes?

*There is no response, so he continues, relieved.*

That's it . . . two very dense Swedes. Anyway, they're driving through Dublin, lost! They're lost on account of them being such stupid Swedes, you know, and one turns to the other and he says, 'I don't think the indicator is working, be a good man and have a look.'

ENGLISHWOMAN  Sexist.

SCOTSMAN  Sorry?

ENGLISHWOMAN  That's sexist, it presupposes that only men are capable of repairing cars.

SCOTSMAN  (*by now rather irritated*) All right, it's two Swedish women then, you know blonde hair, big boobs . . .

ENGLISHWOMAN  Male chauvinist stereotypes.

SCOTSMAN  (*now very pissed off*) There were these two Swedish hermaphrodites driving along, and one says to the other 'Can you get out and see if my indicator is working?' And the other one gets out, looks at the indicator and says 'Yes it is . . . no it isn't . . . yes it is.' (*Laughs*) See? Said it was a killer, didn't I, eh?

*No response. Everyone slowly drifts back to their previous places, looking disgruntled.*

SCOTSMAN  . . . what's up?

LANDLORD  Heard it.

SCOTSMAN  Heard it? When?

LANDLORD  Some fella told it in here yesterday. Only the way he told it, it was two Peruvian unicorns.

# SCOTCH WRATH

## by Andy Hamilton

OWNER Rikki Fulton; GUEST Tony Roper

*A hotel reception desk. A man enters and rings for service. The hotel owner, wearing a kilt and all the gear, comes out to serve him.*

OWNER (*a Scot, wheedling*) A very good evening, sir, and welcome to the Beneagles Hotel. I take it you'll be wanting a room.

GUEST (*English, upper-class*) That's right, for two nights, if you'd be so kind.

OWNER (*stiffening*) Oh . . . you're English.

GUEST Correct.

OWNER In that case, you can't have a room. Good day.

GUEST What?

OWNER You heard.

GUEST But . . . why won't you give me a room?

OWNER Because you're a foreigner.

GUEST I'm not foreign. I'm English.

OWNER You're foreign to me and you're not getting a room, you smelly sassenach scum, so push off.

GUEST Look here, my money's as good as anyone else's. There is no earthly reason why you should refuse me.

OWNER Perfectly true, but you're forgetting one thing . . .

GUEST What's that?

OWNER Culloden.

GUEST Oh don't be ridiculous, that was centuries ago.

OWNER Aye, maybe so, but I've just heard aboot it.

GUEST Now we're both being a bit childish. Surely we are all British?

OWNER Don't you patronise me, you smelly, scummy sassenach, you . . . you're not talking to a tame wee Jock now y'know. I'm a fighting Scot in the tradition of Rob Roy, Bonnie Prince Charlie and Hughie McCorkindale . . . aye there was a man. Went across the world to Argentina and did Scotland proud.

GUEST  What did he do?

OWNER  We're not sure, his case hasnae come up yet.

GUEST  Now look here, you can't turn me away on the grounds of nationality, under English law, it's . . .

OWNER  Oh, aye, English law, well roll on devolution. If I were president of an independent Scotland, you know the first thing I'd do? . . . Rebuild Hadrian's Wall and then electrify it. The next thing I'd do is bring back hanging.

GUEST  Oh yes, for murderers?

OWNER  No, for Englishmen.

GUEST  Oh really!

OWNER (*mimicking*) 'Oh really!' 'I say.' Hark at you, you great poncified Jessie, you stiff-upper-class lah-di-dah twit, get out of my hotel, go on, clear off you great Anglo-wog!

GUEST I am not a wog.

OWNER Look, laddie, as far as I'm concerned, 'wogs begin at Berwick'.

GUEST And what do your other guests say to this?

OWNER Guests? There aren't any guests, you English toadie.

GUEST No guests?

OWNER That's right . . . if things don't improve, I'll maybe have to go back up to Scotland!

# JAPANESE RESTAURANT

## *by John Byrne*

CYRIL McCLUSKEY Rikki Fulton; DEIRDRE Claire Nielson; WAITER Gregor Fisher

*Enter Cyril McCluskey – urbane, sophisticated-looking – and his date for the evening, Deirdre.*
 *A Japanese waiter welcomes them with a bow.*

WAITER Ah, so . . . (*he presents the menu to Deirdre*)

CYRIL (*waving the menus away*) Deirdre dear, when you dine out with Cyril McCluskey, you don't require any of that stuff . . . that's tourist fodder . . . trust me . . . I know your oriental . . . he keeps the best nosh tucked away in the kitchens for the connoisseur . . . the gastronome.

WAITER I take your shoes, sir?

CYRIL See? Now, I could quite easily take off these Hush Puppies and have them done to a turn for the main course but I think we should stick to something a little less outré tonight . . . this is your first time dining out Japanese style, I take it?

96

DEIRDRE Er . . . yes . . .

CYRIL Believe me, you're in for a treat. We could have sweet and sour spaniels or Chow Mein chookies but (*to waiter*) I'll tell you what, China. We'll huv some watter biscuits an' a tin a' bees fur a kick-off, sunshine . . . aw, aye an' bring a cherr fur the burd, eh?

DEIRDRE Oh, Cyril . . .

WAITER (*vexed*) You wish the karate chop! (*Raises hand*)

CYRIL Make it two . . . she'll huv hurs well done . . . mine's rerr . . . an' a coupla nips, eh, pal? (*To Deirdre*) Nips . . . d'ye geddit?!

   *He is felled from behind by the waiter.*

# THE NAUGHTY BITS

•

## ALL TIED UP

### by Quentin Reynolds

**WIFE** Juliet Cadzow; **HUSBAND** Gregor Fisher

*A bedroom. A man (wearing trousers with braces over 'zimitt') is seated on the bed. His feet are tied together. His wife (an ordinary housewife) is tying his hands together.*

**WIFE** Right, whit dae ah dae noo, Willie?

**HUSBAND** (*with lots of leather straps and chains already tied round him*) Tie them tightly Jean so I can't escape. Tighter, tighter.

**WIFE** Whit next, pet?

**HUSBAND** (*even more excited*) That's it – now you can do absolutely anything you like.

**WIFE** Anything?

**HUSBAND** Whatever you want and there's not a thing I can do to stop you . . . Now what are you gonna do?

**WIFE** (*leaving*) Me? I'm going to watch *Eastenders*.

# MASSAGE PARLOUR

## *by Rob Groocock*

CUSTOMER Rikki Fulton; MANAGER Finlay Welsh;
MISS TOMKINS Claire Nielson; PAT Gregor Fisher;
OTHER CUSTOMERS Extras

*A massage parlour, not at all sordid. Behind a reception counter stands a smart clean-cut man in a three-piece suit. Enter a rather untidy man in a donkey jacket. He looks around and two smart-looking men walk out past him, emphasising his untidy appearance.*

CUSTOMER (*to manager in a working-class accent*) Morning.

MANAGER Good morning, sir. Can I be of assistance?

CUSTOMER (*conspiratorially*) Aye, I'd like a massage. (*Giving a 'secret' nod*)

MANAGER Yes. Is this for the purpose of relaxation, weight loss or therapy?

CUSTOMER Oh, relaxation. (*He winks*) Nothing like a massage to relax you eh? (*He winks again and nudges the manager in a deliberate manner – an awkward gesture as the manager is standing behind the counter*) Eh? He, he! (*He nods and winks*)

MANAGER That's a nasty twitch you've got there. If you look at our brochure you'll see that some of our therapy is available on the National Health.

CUSTOMER Oh, aye? (*He looks at the brochure*)

MANAGER Although of course you'll have to pay extra for the private parts.

CUSTOMER Pardon?

MANAGER The private parts of the treatment. As you can see, apart from our NHS work we offer many other services.

CUSTOMER (*brightening up and winking*) Now you're getting the idea. Put me down for a bit of the other.

MANAGER Look, would you mind telling me exactly what you do want?

100

CUSTOMER I've told you . . . I want a massage and some of the extras.

MANAGER What extras?

CUSTOMER (*patiently*) Well how can I put it? Are you married?

MANAGER Well, no, not as such . . .

CUSTOMER Well, supposing you were married to a woman – and you're alone with your wife in the evening. You've been working hard all day to bring home some of life's small luxuries – isn't there some special reward she has for you?

MANAGER Well, yes, I suppose so.

CUSTOMER Well, that's what I want.

MANAGER But we don't sell Ovaltine.

CUSTOMER Look, what if I said *The News of the World*?

MANAGER (*pause*) We don't sell that either.

*Enter a beautiful girl. She sits on the counter and starts to peck at the manager's cheek and whisper in his ear. They giggle.*

CUSTOMER (*pointing at the girl*) Wait a minute! That's what I want, a massage off her!

MANAGER (*smiling patronisingly*) That, I'm afraid, is out of the question. Miss Tomkins here is my secretary. She doesn't do massages.

CUSTOMER (*hopefully*) I'll pay £20.

MANAGER It's not a question of money. Of course if you're really keen, Miss Tomkins has a twin who works here.

CUSTOMER £20, we said.

MANAGER Well, actually, the twin charges £60.

CUSTOMER (*deciding*) Here's £60.

MANAGER (*he rings up the money on the cash till and speaks into the intercom*) Come out here will you, Pat!

*A mountain of a man enters.*

MANAGER There you are, Pat, this gentleman has paid £60 for a massage. He particularly asked for you.

CUSTOMER (*his face changes from lecherous glee to horror, and Pat makes a move to grab him*) Hey, wait a minute, wait a minute. You said it was her twin.

MANAGER True enough, old son. Of course as you can see they aren't identical twins.

CUSTOMER (*as Pat grabs him and drags him away*) But I came here for a kiss and cuddle!

PAT That's all right sir, I'll do anything for money!

*The customer looks terrified as Pat pouts at him and takes him away.*

# THE CAROL SINGER

## *by Bob Black*

CAROL SINGER Rikki Fulton; WOMAN Juliet Cadzow

*A pleasant well-to-do sitting room with expensive furniture, a large set-tee and Christmas decorations. The door bell rings and we hear carol singers halfway through 'Twelve Days of Christmas'. A woman in a negligée and silk robe comes out of bedroom. She is sultry, sexy and seductive. She opens the front door to a middle-aged carol singer with a collecting can. He is a very staid, reserved, inexperienced type – very easily intimidated and scared of women. He smiles and rattles his can.*

CAROL SINGER Good evening. I'm collecting for the South Side Episcopalian –

*The woman kisses him.*

CAROL SINGER . . . Ping-Pong and Scrabble Association. I was wondering if your husband would care to contribute a little some-thing.

*The woman exposes her shoulder.*

CAROL SINGER Well, actually, I was thinking more of 50p.

*The woman pulls him into the room.*

WOMAN My husband's away on business. I'm alone in this great big house . . .

*She bears down on him and the singer backs away, looking shocked and frightened.*

CAROL SINGER Well, forty pence would do.

WOMAN It gets so terribly lonely . . .

CAROL SINGER Twenty . . .?

WOMAN . . . with no one to look after me.

CAROL SINGER I take American Express!

WOMAN . . . and nothing to keep me warm in bed.

*She embraces him, slides down and rests her head on the singer's tummy.*

CAROL SINGER  Well, personally, I use a Snoopy hot water bottle . . .

*He looks back, can't see her, then finds her.*

CAROL SINGER  . . . and woolly socks.

WOMAN  Would you like a drink? I've got Dom Perignon in the bedroom.

CAROL SINGER  Maybe HE'S got 50p!

*The woman rises.*

WOMAN  Don't play games with me. How can you be so cruel? All right, I'll say it. I'll admit it. I'm a nymphomaniac!

*She embraces him again.*

CAROL SINGER  Oh, I'm Sagittarius myself.

*The woman walks him towards the settee.*

WOMAN  I want a man. I NEED a big strong man. Don't you find me attractive?

CAROL SINGER  I don't know.

WOMAN  Why not?

CAROL SINGER  You've steamed up my glasses.

*She rests him on the settee and throws off his glasses.*

WOMAN  You don't need them.

*She throws his can on the settee.*

WOMAN  And you don't need this.

CAROL SINGER  (*trying to get up*) I do, I do. I've still got the other side of the street to knock up – walk up!

*The woman embraces him.*

WOMAN  TAKE ME!

CAROL SINGER  Don't be silly. We can't go carol singing like this!

WOMAN  Take me now. Take me here.

*They fall back on the settee.*

WOMAN  Carry me away.

CAROL SINGER  I can't. The doctor said I mustn't lift anything heavy.

*The singer cries out in pain.*

CAROL SINGER Ooooh! Missus – wait a minute. Ah'm on ma can!

WOMAN Move me! Transport me to the heights of ecstasy.

*The singer gets out from under her and lands on the floor.*

CAROL SINGER Well, I honestly don't think we could get there and back before . . .

WOMAN My husband won't be home for weeks.

CAROL SINGER Yes, but the carol singers have only got half a chorus to go. They, they'll wonder where I am.

*She comes to him and starts pulling him by the scarf.*

WOMAN Forget them. Forget everything! Come with me. To the bedroom. To the bedroom!

*The doorbell rings, the woman goes into the bedroom and the singer hauls himself up.*

CAROL SINGER Oh well, I really must be toddling along now. Got lots more fifty p's to have . . . to get. And I like to get home in time for *The Beechgrove Garden*. I'll maybe call round later when you've got some loose change – and had an Askit.

*The woman appears in silhouette. She drops her gown and the singer is nonplussed. The door bell rings again. He goes to the door.*

CAROL SINGER (*shouting out of the door*) Right, lads. From the top – ONE MORE TIME!

*The singer closes the front door and heads for the bedroom, throwing off his anorak and pausing only long enough to put a fifty pence coin in the collection box.*

# THE LETTER

## *by Quentin Reynolds*

HUSBAND Rikki Fulton; WIFE Juliet Cadzow

*The kitchen of a typical house at breakfast time.*

*The husband is reading a newspaper. His wife has a small bundle of letters beside her. She picks up the first envelope, opens it and takes out a letter.*

*The husband glances over from behind the paper.*

HUSBAND  Who's your letter from?

WIFE  Hilary. What a scrawl!

> *She grimaces. Having trouble reading the handwriting, she leans over to show part of the letter to her husband.*

WIFE  Would you say that was an 'o' or an 'i'?

HUSBAND  *(barely interested)* Looks like an 'o' . . .

WIFE  *(appalled)* Oh, God, my brother's shot himself!

# THE SHOPPER

## by Bob Black

NEWSAGENT Tony Roper; CUSTOMER Rikki Fulton

*A newsagent's shop with a man serving behind the counter. Another man, a customer, stands facing him. As the customer states what he wants, the newsagent puts the appropriate magazines on the counter.*

CUSTOMER I'll have a copy of *Men Only* . . . *Playboy* . . . *Hot Sex* . . . *Nudes Galore* . . . *Bare Scuddy Women* . . . and *Rude Nudes and Dirty Bisoms* . . .

*The newsagent has piled them on the counter. The man looks round in a shifty manner now, suddenly very self-consious and embarrassed, lowering his voice.*

Oh, and, er . . . a *Sunday Post. (Embarrassed)* Honest, it's not for me. It's for a friend.

# TECHNOLOGY

## by Rikki Fulton

POLICEMAN Gregor Fisher; V/O RADIO Juliet Cadzow

*A policeman with 183 on his shoulder strides along the street. We see him only from the waist up. His two-way radio starts to crackle.*

V/O RADIO Control to C. Charlie 183.

*He takes it out and acknowledges the call.*

POLICEMAN 183. Go ahead.

V/O RADIO Your fly's open!

*In great embarrassment, the policeman looks down, quickly puts the radio away, stuffs in his shirt, zips up his fly, and looking round to make sure no one has seen him, hurries off.*

# BACK STREET SEX CHANGE

## by Laurie Rowley

NURSE Andrea Miller; DOCTOR Rikki Fulton;
RITA HAYWORTH Tony Roper

*A fairly seedy doctor's office. The doctor sits behind his desk, looking at page three of a daily tabloid. The nurse enters, chewing gum and filing her nails.*

NURSE Doctor, Miss Rita Hayworth to see you.

DOCTOR Oh hell, tell her I'm out, tell her . . .

*Rita Hayworth enters. Rita is a man dressed as a woman and has stubble and a small moustache. The nurse leaves.*

DOCTOR . . . Ahhh Miss Hayworth, nice to see you. Please take a seat.

RITA I want a word with you, Dr Nogood.

DOCTOR Certainly Miss Hayworth. What seems to be the trouble?

RITA I'm not entirely satisfied with my sex change operation – I want my money back.

DOCTOR What? I don't recall treating such a beautiful woman. Are you sure . . .?

RITA You did the operation last week, remember? And I demand my money back.

DOCTOR (*looking through his card index*) 'Scuse me . . . Hayworth . . . Hayworth . . . Ahh Hayworth, here we are. (*Reading from the card*) Rita Hayworth, once known as Arthur Johnstone. You know, Miss Hayworth, looking at you it's astounding. If I weren't the one who carried out your operation I'd swear you'd been born a woman. Have a cigar.

*He hands Rita a box of Havanas.*

RITA (*getting out a pipe*) No thanks, I'll stick to this.

DOCTOR In fact I don't think I've ever seen a woman look more beautiful, Miss Hayworth . . . or may I call you Rita?

RITA You can call me Arthur like everyone else still does.

DOCTOR You know you look so attractive when you get mad, but try not to get over-excited. Remember what I told you, you must take things easy until the new hormones start to take effect.

RITA Oh they're taking effect all right – I've never had a beard before.

DOCTOR Surely you've had a beard.

RITA Not growing around my navel!

DOCTOR A temporary side effect, or front effect even, Miss Hayworth. It's what we call the 'Ugly Duckling' stage. Give it a month and you'll eventually blossom into the magnificent White Swan of womanhood.

RITA You mean I'll grow an orange beak???

DOCTOR Ha, ha! No Miss Hayworth, of course not . . . *(aside)* webbed feet perhaps, but . . . but you don't mean to tell me that with such an aura of mysterious feminine charm you haven't received a few admiring glances from the male population? A few wolf-whistles perhaps?

RITA Well there was one chap . . .

DOCTOR And what did he give you?

RITA  A suspended sentence, and that's why I want my money back. I want a refund.

DOCTOR  Well, if that's the way you feel, Miss Hayworth.

RITA  Yes it is, I feel as though I've been cheated, I don't look like a woman, and worst of all . . .

DOCTOR  What?

RITA  (*bringing out a coconut shell from her blouse*) . . . these coconut shells make me itch.

DOCTOR  They're bounty. Miss Hayworth, I can assure you – you are one of the most attractive women I've ever met. In fact if it weren't for the circumstances, I think . . . I think I'd ask you to marry me.

RITA  Oh Doctor – do you really mean that?

DOCTOR  I certainly do. I'd marry you tomorrow if it weren't for one thing.

RITA  What's that?

*The doctor gets up and walks around the desk. He wears high-heeled shoes and a skirt.*

DOCTOR  My operation didn't work either . . .


# FLASHERS

## *by Paul Eldergill*

SERGEANT Gregor Fisher; WOMAN Claire Nielson;
FOUR MEN Extras


*A police station interior. A police sergeant is talking to a middle-aged spinster.*

SERGEANT  We're ready, Miss Ridley. Now, if you recognise the man who flashed at you in the High Street, just point him out to me.

WOMAN  Very well, Sergeant.

*She walks down a line of men all holding their raincoats open. At each one she looks at his face and then at his lower regions. She has a different expression at each one. The last man but one is very well-built but her expression is one of disappointment. The last man is very small in stature but by her expression he is very gifted in other departments.*

*She returns to the Sergeant.*

SERGEANT  Well, Miss Ridley, did you spot him?

WOMAN  No I didn't, I'm sorry.

SERGEANT  Oh.

WOMAN  Same time tomorrow as usual, Sergeant?

SERGEANT  (*fed up*) Very well, Miss Ridley, same time tomorrow.


# THE VAMPIRE
## *by Bob Black*

### DRACULA Tony Roper; MAN Extra


*A bedroom at night. Very dark and shadowy. A man and woman are lying in bed. The man sighs, unable to sleep. He gets out of bed and leaves the room in his pyjamas.*

*Suddenly the curtains of the French windows billow out and a vampire steps into the room. He has a white face, red lips and a bat-like cloak. Eerie music builds . . .*

*He hisses evilly and spreads his arms and cloak. He stalks round the room for a moment, then notices the woman in bed, and looks hungry and lustful!*

*He goes over to her, crouches beside her and leans over.*

*The eerie music reaches its climax as he bites her neck.*

*Suddenly there is a loud farting noise and a rush of escaping air!*

*The vampire straightens up, and pulls a rapidly deflating inflatable woman from under the bedclothes!*

112

# THE REV. I. M. JOLLY

•

## LIFT UP YOUR HEARTS
### by Rikki Fulton

REV. I. M. JOLLY  Hello! What sort of day have you had? Has it been a good day? Has it been happy for you? Did something wonderful happen to you – like your train coming in on time, or your electricity bill being less than you thought it would be? I'm joking, of course! No. Far more important than 'What sort of day have YOU had' . . . is the question, 'What have you done to make this day better for others?' I believe, you see, that it is more important to make someone else happy, than to be happy yourself. It is essential when you are having a good day  to share the joy of it with our fellow men.

For myself, I have had a helluva day! In fact, the whole week has been something of a pain in the arm for me. I think, perhaps, I pulled a muscle the other night when conducting the choir. The choir! That is a laugh. Two old men and a snotty-nosed youth from an approved school. We foster him, you know. It's like living with a piranha fish. Then on Monday I had to clear up the whole area in front of the pulpit. With shovel and wheelbarrow I laboured long. All because Mrs McCandlish, the coalman's wife, had this remarkable idea of sitting on top of her husband's Clydesdale and doing the Sermon on the Mount. Well, whether the horse was embarrassed or frightened, I don't know, but . . .

Anyway, all that carry-on with the shovel and the wheelbarrow put my back out, and between that and my arm – I was up all night. The pain was excruciating! I sprayed it with liniment, but there was just

113

no improvement. You know that awful way when it doesn't matter how you lie, you just cannot get relief. I tried this way and that. Eventually I ended up sort of kneeling with one arm up the chimney and the other under the pillow, my head in the bedside cabinet, one leg outside the bed and the other across my good lady. She being a decisive woman and in some doubt as to my intentions, rose up and belted me one.

I think it was at this point the dog was sick. Probably the smell of the liniment. Not that I mind the poor beast bringing up his dinner – it's just that, of course, he would sleep at MY side. By the time I got that lot cleaned up it was time to rise and shine . . . when suddenly there was a ring at the front door and when I opened it, there was this sweet little girl selling lucky white heather.

My case comes up next Tuesday. Goodnight.

# KEEP SMILING

## by Rikki Fulton

REV. I. M. JOLLY Hello! D'you ever get the feeling that life's just one great disaster area? That, some mornings, you just shouldn't get up? That everybody and everything is against you? . . . So do I! Yes, it'll maybe surprise you to know that I'm not always the chirpy happy-go-lucky chap I make myself out to be.

So this is my message to all of you: 'Keep smiling!' It's worth remembering what Plato once said: 'Quae ferunt vitia, mores sunt.' I don't know what it means, but it's worth remembering.

Of course, as I've said before, I am lucky to have a very dear wife. I don't think you could get a dearer wife! Ephesia. She's a remarkable woman. On Monday she just made up her mind, went into the hairdresser and had her hair cut off. She came out looking like a new man. Mind you I have to admit she's always had a sort of masculine appearance. I think it's the moustache. Indeed for the first three years of our courtship I was convinced I was still going out with the boys. But like me, she has this great ability to see the funny side of things. When I told her, for instance, that old Mr McCorkindale had died intestate, she remarked that it was probably because he hadn't had enough roughage in his diet! I have to laugh. It's as much as my life's worth.

Not that there was much to laugh about last week. The church concert wasn't exactly what you'd describe as the acme of show business. To start with, the grand piano fell off the stage and became an upright. Then part of the curtain came away during Mrs McCandlish's solo. I would have come away myself if I'd had the chance. Although I was quite glad I stayed when almost immediately a piece of scenery fell and tore off the front part of her dress. It was pure irony that it happened while she was singing 'These are my Mountains'.

Still we made a clear profit of ninety-six pence which has been put to the Roof Repair Fund – and that means we can buy another slate.

Then on Sunday old Mr Pettigrew had a disaster with his organ. It's an antiquated old thing that should have gone on the rubbish heap long ago. Not unlike old Mr Pettigrew. Honestly, the time that's spent between hymns when he fiddles with his feet and changes his combinations . . .!

Anyway, it's old Mrs Agnew that pumps for him. And it's a generally accepted fact that there's just nobody that can pump like Mrs Agnew. She's quite the strongest pumper we've ever had in the church. But then she's been pumping on and off for over sixty years and it's obviously something that comes naturally to her. Oh, people come from far and near when word gets round that Mrs Agnew is going to pump. Believe me when Mrs Agnew pumps, you know somebody has pumped! However, most unfortunately last Sunday during evensong Mrs Agnew was pumping away with her usual zeal when, quite suddenly, her lever broke. Just came away in her hand. Right in the middle of a pump. Not that it bothered Mrs Agnew, but it certainly put the wind up old Mr Pettigrew. So, the moral is: 'Wherever you be – let your sense of humour prevail.'

Goodnight.

# EPHESIA AND HER FRIENDS

## *by Rikki Fulton*

THE REV I. M. JOLLY  Hello! Well, here I am again, positively flushed with consti – anticipation at the thought of us prancing merrily, hand in hand, into yet another New Year.

What delights are in store for us?

Meeting Jimmy Savile on the 5.35 to Edinburgh. Meeting Jimmy Savile anywhere.

But enough of this couthy, homespun humour. I've had one or two letters since I last spoke to you. There was an interesting one from a woman who couldn't make up her mind if she should seek a separation – and if she did, would her husband offer some sort of uplift? So I sent her one of these cross-your-heart brassières. That way, as I pointed out, she could get support, uplift and separation all in one go.

My good lady, Ephesia, has one of these brassières. Not a small size, I must admit. In fact, it's not the first time she's forgotten her shopping basket and brought home a couple of stone of potatoes in it.

Of course, this year nothing would do, but my dear wife had to enter for the Glasgow marathon. She was doing quite well, too. Head down, pushing herself along like a hippopotamus in labour, when suddenly she experienced a head-on collision with a double-decker bus.

The bus was a write-off and Ephesia was knocked more unconscious than usual at my feet. Well, the people immediately crowded round us. It was awfully embarrassing for her. Not one of the men would volunteer to give her the kiss of life. Not even when I offered them money. By this time she had lost her jumper. It had flown off into a field and some people were using it as a refreshment tent. Then the bus driver rushed up and looked down at her lying there, topless.

'Oh,' he says, 'that's terrible.' I had to agree with him.

'What do you think we ought to do?' he says.

And some wag in the crowd says, 'If I were you, mate, Ah would treat it as a double roundabout.'

117

But our really testing time was just the other week when we held our winter fair. It wasn't exactly a howling success. More what you might call an unmitigated disaster.

Since we're a mining community we duly elected our Miss Coalface of 1984. It was supposed to have been Big Annie McPartland, but she was pregnant and couldn't get into the frock. So we had to rope in Mrs McCandlish, the coalman's wife. Well, I just can't stand that woman. She gives me a pain in the armpit. Always talking. In fact, she reminds me of one of these Venus's flytraps. The only time her mouth's shut is when there's food in it.

The next thing that happened was that old Mr Bampot, who is ninety-three and pretty frail, entered the grass-cutting competition with a Flymo. He was shot down over Pittenweem.

But the final catastrophe was the dinner dance later that night. We had the dance all right, but nobody had remembered to organise the dinner. So Mrs McCandlish had to rush down to the Chinese Carry-Out for fifty-nine portions of haddock and chips. Well, we weren't sure what happened, but apparently the wee Chinaman said something she took exception to, and she started battering the poor man over the head with her umbrella. Fortunately she desisted when someone explained that what he had actually said was 'Fish off!'

Oh, and there was worse to come. This raving lunatic rushed into the shop and started belting the McCandlish woman with a black pudding. Honestly, can you imagine such rampant idiocy – such blundering stupidity? My lawyer says I should plead diminished responsibility.

Goodnight.


# DECK OF CARDS
## by Rikki Fulton

THE REV. I. M. JOLLY Hello! And it came to pass that the skies darkened, the trees bent in the wind, the heavens opened and it rained for forty days and forty nights. So much for the summer!

Typically, we'll all be looking to next year, and hoping things will be better. But at this time of year we should also take a look behind us, keeping alive some of our HAPPIEST memories. For example I can remember the day I first met my wife Ephesia.

That's maybe not the best example, but still . . .

I had been officiating at a Christmas wedding in Falkirk. It was a mixed marriage – she came from Edinburgh and he came from Glasgow. Anyway, during the reception, I met Ephesia just outside the ladies toilet. She was going in just as I was coming out. And suddenly she held a small bunch of mistletoe over my head and kissed me. Of course I kissed her back. I certainly wasn't going to kiss her face! But it's amazing to think that we've been inseparable ever since. Like chewing gum on the sole of life.

That was also the year I started making my hospital visits. Going round the wards, giving uplifting, cheery little talks to the elderly patients. How often I've had cause to be grateful that I went in time – so many of them passed away just after I'd been there.

And it was at New Year one year when I was returning home by train that a fight broke out in my compartment. Three young men quarrelled over a game of poker, and suddenly one of them began driving his knee again and again into the groin of an innocent passenger. I had to intervene. After all, it was my groin!

But I took the opportunity of explaining how a deck of cards can offer us a great deal of spiritual insight. For example, when I see the ace, two and three I think of young Jason McClumpha who was caught moonlighting and drawing his dole at the same time.

He was called before three DHSS inspectors who asked him his name.

'Joseph,' he replied cheekily.

'What's your wife's name?' they asked him.

'Mary,' he replied.

'Where do you live?' they asked him.

'Nazareth,' he said.

'Well, Joseph,' they said, 'just you go home to Nazareth and tell Mary that "The Three Wise Men" have stopped your burroo money!'

The four reminds me of the number of people in the congregation at last week's Evening Service. The five and six the fifty-six pence we took in the collection.

When I see the seven, eight and nine, I remember that was the number of the hotel bedroom where I spent my honeymoon. It was absolute bliss, even though Ephesia had had to stay at home with a headache. I was young then and quite daring. I asked the chambermaid to bring me early morning tea – at four o' clock! I was still awake when the knock came and a porter brought in the tea. 'Where's the chambermaid?' I asked somewhat disappointedly.

'I don't know, sir,' he replied. 'But the teapot's made in Birmingham.'

The ten makes me think of the choir – ten wise virgins, I've never believed in foolish virgins. They always seemed a contradiction in terms. And then Jack, of course, old Jack Bampot, organist and choirmaster whose renderings on the organ get more and more like *Name that Tune*.

The queen is, of course, my good lady, Ephesia, who's been on a diet for six weeks and all she's lost is her temper. However, this time she has a real incentive to get her weight down as she's been offered the title role in the dramatic society's stage version of *Moby Dick*.

And finally, there is the king which I see as my father who taught me the real meaning of TRUTH. My father works in the mill at Luncarty, and we lived in a little cottage which had an outside toilet about a hundred yards away standing at the edge of the river. One day our toilet was found upside down in the water. My father called me to him: 'I am going to ask you a question, but before I do I want you to remember the story of George Washington who cut down his father's favourite cherry tree and who, when asked, declared, "I cannot tell a lie, father. It was I who cut down the cherry tree." And his father rewarded him. Now,' said my father, 'what can you tell me about the toilet?'

120

'I cannot tell a lie,' I cried. 'I pushed the toilet into the river!'

Well, he nearly murdered me! I've never had such a thrashing in my life. I cried out in despair. 'But father,' I said, 'you told me that George Washington said "I cut down the cherry tree" and his father rewarded him!'

'I know,' said my father, 'but George Washington's father was not sitting in the cherry tree when it was cut down!'

Goodnight.

# 1984

## *by Rikki Fulton*

THE REV. I. M. JOLLY  Hello! Well, that's another year we've managed to put in. (*He blows a party squeaker*) I'll bet that surprised you ... It certainly put the wind up ME! I suppose I get a wee bit skittish at this time of the year. I've really got to keep a tight rein on myself or I'd do something outrageous like rushing into the BBC and shouting 'Scottish television!!!!' And it's not that I'm all that happy about it being New Year. It's just that I'm that damn glad to see the back of the OLD one!

So here we are – trembling at the gate of 1984. A year so vividly described by George Orwell in his book called, er, in that book he wrote. And what nonsense it contained. What a load of crass stupidity. 'Big Brother's watching you!' Big Sister maybe – but Big Brother?!

I don't know about you, but looking forward to another year with its new challenges and problems always gives me a feeling of – what's the word . . .?
NAUSEA!

Anyway, what sort of festive season have you had? Did you have a happy time or did your relations come to visit you? Did you get just what you've always wanted for Christmas? Did your tree stay up? Did your fairy lights work?

But enough of this pawkiness!

Our own season was something of a mixed bag. And speaking of the wife, Ephesia invited her entire family this year and cooked Christmas dinner for them. I really had to hand it to her. After all these years she got her own back at one fell swoop!

There have been all sorts of goings-on in the parish. Our local flasher came to see me in a very distressed state. Apparently he'd developed a terrible inferiority complex because people kept laughing at him.

Our organist, old Mr Bampot, fell off his organ in September – fractured his treble and damaged his combinations. And he was no sooner out and about again when he was struck by a second tragedy. It seems he'd received two Christmas presents which were identical, only different. One was a set of that waterproof underwear. I don't know what you call them, but it's got something to do with what old people wear on the continent. And the other present was a set of thermal underwear that were so old-fashioned you had to plug them into the mains.

Well, it seems he was wearing them BOTH at the Watch Night Service and – well, we don't really know what happened. I think maybe he got a wee bit excited playing Handel's *Water Music* . . . anyway there was this tremendous flash, and the next thing we knew we were all standing there singing 'He is Gone Beyond the Skies' – unaccompanied. So it's not been a happy year for us. Especially when we remember that we'd not long had the organ overhauled. But now, a prayer:

'Oh Lord, teach us to have chastity and restraint. But not just yet!'

Goodnight.

# MERRY CHRISTMAS
## *by Rikki Fulton*

THE REV. I. M. JOLLY Hello! Death, disaster, famine, disease – the poll tax! I suppose some of you sometimes think that life's not worth living.

Oh, so do I.

What a Christmas! For one thing we couldn't find the fairy lights. Searched everywhere. Then eventually we discovered the dog had taken them into his kennel. He's just a wee dog with legs like a fox terrier and a face like a boxer. A wee bit like Barry McGuigan. But there in his kennel he had the fairy lights all strung out in neat little loops. Ephesia was very impressed. 'There you are,' she said to me.

'The bloomin' dog's a damn sight cleverer than you are.' I said, 'He's not so clever. He can't make them work either!'

Then the fairy fell off the top of the Christmas tree. Though what he was doing there in the first place, I don't know.

Then I christened a child Thingby McClafferty. Thingby! The mother couldn't remember what she'd decided to call her. When I took the babe in my arms I said to the mother, 'But this child's head is already wet.' She said, 'I know. You're holding it upside down.' I must say I had wondered about the enormous grin on its face.

And this year we had decided to put up an illuminated Christmas message above the church door. Unfortunately Mercedes McClumpha, the session secretary who would have to make the arrangements, wasn't at that meeting. So I went round to her house and popped a note through her letter box giving the text of the message and the dimensions of the sign. Apparently she collapsed in a dead heap when she read the note for it said, 'Unto us a child is born. Eight feet high and five feet wide'!

So, it was all a time of frustration and disappointment for me, but I long ago learned to laugh off such irritations. It rather reminded me of that other ancient parable of misadventure which you may remember.

And lo, there were ten vestal virgins. Five were wise virgins and five were foolish virgins. And the five wise virgins were elderly and irritable for they had been wise for many years, and it was getting on their wick. And it came to pass that these ten virgins were called upon to attend a bridal feast with their lamps. And during the celebrations the five foolish virgins partook of the good wine in abundance and one by one their lamps went out.

And when they awoke they said unto the wise virgins, 'Give us of your oil that we might replenish our lamps.'

And the wise virgins spake unto them saying, 'Get thyselves knotted. Go into the marketplace, get thyselves a trolley, and purchase that which you need.'

So the five foolish virgins set off, but came unto the wrong marketplace. And they spake unto a Sadducee who was there, saying, 'We are five foolish virgins who need our wicks trimmed and our oil replenishing.'

'Go ye to yonder house,' replied the Sadducee. 'Knock thrice upon the door and ask for Obadiah.'

The foolish virgins did as they were bidden and approaching a small door, knocked three times. Whereupon it was opened unto them and they spake saying, 'We are five foolish virgins.'

'Thou hast come to the right place,' said Obadiah.

And, lo, they entered – otherwise they would have bumped their heads on the door. And having no light, they had to sit in the dark with the boys. Which was very foolish, for though they kept their hands on their lamps, they were soon well oiled.

And it came to pass that when the five foolish virgins returned to the feast they spake unto the wise virgins saying, 'Rejoice, sisters, for we are not the foolish virgins that ye knew. For not only have we lost our FOOLISHNESS, but we have lost our lamps as well.'

Goodnight.

# THE NEW YEAR
## *by Rikki Fulton*

THE REV. I. M. JOLLY Hello! Well, that's another year gone! Any minute now we'll be facing a new, vigorous, thrilling, challenging, dynamic era. I don't know about you, but I'm incredibly moved. I can hardly speak for the turbulent emotions which are surging through my body, if you'll pardon the expression. I just don't know when I've been so excited. My wife, Ephesia, says she can't remember either.

And so the bells'll be ringing out their joyous message of hope and cheer and goodwill towards men and love thy neighbour, and ships too, on the Clyde, will set their sirens screaming and, what with the bells and the screaming sirens, a good New Year will be upon us. Not to mention a good earache as well!

And what sort of year have you had? Has it been a good year? Has it been happy? Has it been successful? But enough of this waggishness! For myself, I try not to think of this past year as having been an uphill struggle, hardship, suffering, gloom and despondency. I like to think of it more as sheer misery.

Mind you, it has been an interesting year in many ways. In the last twelve months I have been to no less than 147 funerals! Not in an official capacity, you understand. It's really just a wee kind of hobby

of mine. And, of course, if it's a morning 'do' – it always saves you making your own lunch. Ephesia enjoys them, too, for she likes meeting people. Even if it is too late!

In the Spring, Ephesia, forever seeking ways to harness her great energy, started up a soup kitchen for down and outs. Unfortunately, the only people who kept turning up were her relatives. But then in no time word got round, and my family turned up as well.

Later in the year she came with me when I went to London as a member of a working party from the Motherwell Municipal Home for Maladjusted Ministers. Or as we call it, Mmhmm!

Ephesia was particularly interested in the problems of vice in the Big City and during her research in Soho invited a number of us to view a typical pornographic film. Well, I mean, honestly – four-letter words, nudity, violence and sleazy sex!?

I enjoyed it!!

And to put your minds at rest, I can assure you that it's something that quickly loses its appeal. I mean, I saw it fourteen times and I know.

126

Anyway the old year is now in the past. We must look to the future and Ephesia and I do wish you whatever's coming to you in the New Year! And to you if you live alone – mind your back!

But I leave you with this thought. Look to your fellow man, your neighbour. Love him, and trust him – he will not fail you – and together you will go forward to a bigger, better, brighter future – than ever before. If you can believe that . . . you can believe ANYTHING.

# HIGHLIGHTS OF MY YEAR

## by Rikki Fulton

THE REV. I. M. JOLLY Hello! You're probably all sitting out there saying, 'What's he got to be so cheery about?' Well, don't be taken in by this air of devil-may-care abandon. Like many of you, I'm sure I often sit here and suffer. I got some ointment for it, but . . . Anyway, what sort of year have you had? Has it been a good year? Has it been full of happiness, excitement – joy?!

That must be the biggest laugh since the Tay Bridge Disaster. On the other hand, speaking personally, I've had a helluva year.

To start with, we had a terrible accident in the church choir. Old Mr Jamieson, who sings soprano for us, tried to reach a top C and burst his braces.

Then Mrs Pattison, our church organist, got a wee bit over-excited playing a complicated Bach Fugue and ruined her combinations. But there was a lesson in all of this. It brought home to me what my old professor used to say. 'Don't waste time and energy thinking about yourself and getting depressed,' he said. 'Look around you. Think of others. And get depressed about THEM!'

I don't know about you, but I hate New Year. Isn't it funny how you always look back and think of something you wish you hadn't done? Speaking of the wife, Ephesia wasn't quite herself for a while. It was great while it lasted, but . . . Actually, I think it started with the World Cup. She enjoyed it tremendously, but she found it pretty tiring. She was playing right-back for Poland.

Of course I can always tell when Ephesia's under a lot of pressure, being so close to her. Oh, there are lots of signs. Just little things like coming home and finding my slippers waiting for me – in the fridge.

Mind you, there was a highlight to the year. The Women's Guild decided to have their church outing in Majorca this year. Old Clem Sinclair had managed to get what he called 'a very good deal' from Fly-by-Night Tours – £35 a head and find your own way to Barcelona.

Well, if you'd seen the plane . . . We had to give it a shove down the hill to get it started. Actually the trip wouldn't have been so bad if it hadn't been for these two kids running up and down the aisle laughing and shouting. Oh, I soon put a stop to that. I just opened a door and told them to play outside.

Oh, if you could have heard the mother. What she didn't call me! That was all right too, though. She went out to look for them.

The Hotel Basura, as it was called, was a huge place. Over 400 beds. Unfortunately they were all in the one room. But there was plenty to do and I could see that Ephesia was beginning to relax. In fact, one day she came down to the beach topless! I must say I didn't approve and said so. So she put the wig back on. There was a lovely 3½-hole golf course there, too. I hadn't played golf for years and suggested to Ephesia that we play a round. But she had a headache as usual. Anyway, now she's back, refreshed, and has thrown herself into her social work again among the misfits of society, the bewildered and feeble-minded. Or as I call them – her family.

And that's the old year gone. I'm sure next year will be much better. Wouldn't bank on it, mind you. But, you know, I always remember what my dear old father used to say to me. 'Angela,' he would say (he'd a terrible memory for names. At least that's what he said!). 'Angela,' he would say, 'no matter what muck life throws at you, smile. Keep smiling, because, let's face it, things could be worse.' And that's what I did. I just smiled. And you know, my dear old father was right. Things ARE a bloody sight worse.